Morning Light

"Kane weaves a threnody of desire and guilt . . . David's invocation of Echo and Narcissus as a parallel to his relationship with Emily gives a pointed hint at the battle between lust and love that reverberates throughout . . . enjoyable reading."

 – *Publishers Weekly*

"Kane weaves an intriguing web between the flawed, complex characters . . . story of loss, ethics and forbidden love."

 – *Kirkus Reviews*

"a poignant novel . . . examines long-buried memories and unsolved mysteries . . . [that] comes full circle from loss and longing to passionate, obsessive love and, eventually, a sense of self."

 – D. Donovan, *Midwest Book Review*

"Part literary memoir, part poignant psychological drama, this haunting love story explores the secrets of attraction and the mysteries of obsession—a boy's coming-of-age, and one woman's search for love and success in a year of intense achievement and painful loss."

 – Aloi, *Guiltless Reading*

"Kane shows sensitivity to language and story in this revealing book—I couldn't put it down."

 – Ina Bray, librarian and former chair of the King County Arts Commission

"... a modern woman's search for love and fulfillment, Holland Kane sheds light on the dark places our dreams can carry us, places we never meant to go."

    – Carol Orlock, award-winning novelist

"A beautifully written novel!"

    – Sara Strauss, *Style & Books*

Winter Reeds

"Holland Kane writes fiction that will make you think."

    – Billy Squier, American rock musician

"... filled with unexpected twists and turns ... imminent danger ... mysteries and corruption come together ... the pacing of the unfolding mystery is satisfyingly quick and easy to read. Kane spins a fascinating web of discoveries and intrigue, and the surprises don't stop until the very end. A gripping tale of how some secrets can't be buried."

    – *Kirkus Reviews*

"In a novel filled with intrigue and mystery, Holland Kane has woven a dark enchantment—one you won't want to escape."

    – Carol Orlock, award-winning novelist

"*Winter Reeds* provides a powerful first novel and tells of documentary filmmaker Mike Harrison, who moves to a remote northwest town to research an unsolved arson that left two dead. He's intent on solving the mystery—but standing in the way is a popular town sheriff who uses his deputies and traffic cameras as tools to keep outsiders from exposing the small town's secrets."

    – D. Donovan, *Midwest Book Review*

CAR PALACE

Gediminas Trimakas

Also by Gediminas Trimakas as Holland Kane

Winter Reeds
Morning Light
Deer Creek

CAR PALACE

A Memoir

GEDIMINAS TRIMAKAS

rumor house books

Car Palace

© 2017 Gediminas Trimakas

Rumor House Books
6029 95th Pl SW
Mukilteo, WA 98275
rumorhousebooks.com

For more information about this book, visit **www.trimakasauthor.com**

 www.facebook.com/gediminas.trimakas

Edition ISBNs

Trade Paperback: 978-0-9858293-8-4

Hardcover: 978-0-9858293-2-2

E-book: 978-0-9858293-9-1

First Edition 2017

This edition was prepared for printing by
The Editorial Department
7650 E. Broadway, #308
Tucson, Arizona 85710
www.editorialdepartment.com

Cover design by Kelly Leslie
Cover photo by Gediminas Trimakas
Book interior design by Morgana Gallaway

This book is for Donna

FOREWORD

DONNA AND I SET OUT ON OUR LIFE TOGETHER AS TEENAG-ers, married young, and then marched and danced and sang our way along the Yellow Brick Road looking to find the Wizard of Oz. We didn't have Dorothy to guide us, or the Scarecrow, the Tin Man, and the Cowardly Lion to keep us company, but we too could have used more brain, more heart, and more courage at different times in our lives.

A dozen Totos accompanied us too—affectionate, cuddly, and sometimes moody dogs, often at least two at a time to keep each other company—along with a capuchin monkey, many pet birds, several cats, and after a time, and to our good fortune, two children. We hopped and skipped and picked ourselves up when we tripped. Not so delightfully as Dorothy out of Kansas, but lifted by a whirlwind nonetheless.

As immigrants from Lithuania, we landed separately in the USA, me in Brooklyn and Donna in Philadelphia, and started our Great American journey as refugees, DPs—displaced persons fleeing war.

You can think of *Car Palace* as a piece of travel writing. Off to the side of the Yellow Brick Road were many smaller roads that we were tempted to try. Some were badly marked—bordered by social anxiety, class distinction, and gender bias. Some roads were privately owned, gated, guarded by entitled elites, walled off by family money and inherited wealth. Other roads were restricted, but could be entered after ambitious effort. There were several grand roads that we traveled that in retrospect appear gaudy. Roads that allowed individuals of slender means such as us to dream large.

These are experiences worth sharing, and scenes worth showing. Some scenes picture America's Main Street, where modest success gives meaning to lives lived on the edge. There are scenes from a marriage too—some of it adventurous.

Becoming is part of the American creed; change is our foundational text. It's how we measure handfuls of confusion and shape them into purpose, looking for meaning as moral beings and determined actors staging the invention of our lives.

A mild disclaimer first: I changed names, gender, and identifying details of some individuals, renamed organizations and altered locations to preserve the privacy of people who are not known to the public. I'm grateful to others who wanted me to record our interviews. Any professional or legal information imbedded within the book serves as background and is not intended as legal advice. The opinions and reservations I express in this book may differ from the memories and recollections and opinions of other participants, all of them good people. The rivalry, the frictions, the silences—successes and failures—and the many doubts as to The Road Not Taken is part of the story.

Memory is both beautiful and strange and often difficult to evaluate. Annie Dillard, Toni Morrison, Alfred Kazin, and many others, have offered observations on how to confront the difficulties. Some of these are collected in William Zinsser's book, *Inventing the Truth*. His masterful title describes the process well. Our emotional watershed moments remain intensely present across many years, but the narrative details—the words spoken, the time of day, the color of the sky, the amount of rain in the gutter, and how loudly the door slammed—grow hazy. Antonia Fraser in her memoir *My History* takes several lines from the play *Old Times*, written by her husband, Harold Pinter, to explain: "There are things I remember that may never have happened but as I recall them so they take place."

In this tangled web of memory, research, observation, intuition, invention, and hindsight, I've placed my own memoir. Where I've added narrative detail to the unstable mix of recall and impression, I did so in the service of expressing emotions that remain vivid. F. Scott Fitzgerald's Gatsby exclaimed, "Can't repeat the past?...Why of course you can!" This is my attempt to repeat the past.

1

ALL NIGHT THE RAIN FELL, SPLATTERING THE CEDAR ROOF in a steady pattern of muted sounds. The climate is temperate in Seattle. The clouds have parted to reveal a full moon. "We don't have to do it," Donna says. Her eyes shine in the darkness, and her voice is intimate. It's two in the morning and we're standing on the deck of our house, holding on to the weathered cedar rail. Fate has flung us from the eastern shore of the Baltic Sea to Puget Sound, a passage that has taken many miles and years. Puget Sound connects us to the oceans of the world, the bays and estuaries, and the seas that reach back to our Lithuanian past, severed from our lives by what was once known as the Iron Curtain.

We hear the chimes we've hung from the eaves of the house. The largest among them is tolling as we slip the moment and enter the timelessness of dreams, the scents and sounds and sights from the past—the sweet scent of fresh cut hay, the sound of birds, and the sight of fields and flowers.

In these moments of reverie our imaginations rely on the photographs our parents left us, showing their lives before we were born. In one photo, my father, the Lithuanian first counsel to Sweden, and my mother attend a diplomatic reception. My father is splendid in white tie. From the left lapel and across his chest cascade four medals honoring his services. He's a young man who's earned his PhD in agronomy and economics from the Université Catholique de Lille in France. My slim mother is elegant in a black evening dress. She's caught in mid-gesture, her cigarette holder raised. A golden asp suggesting Cleopatra's fate girds the holder's amber. The cigarette remains unlit.

No one at this gathering of diplomats knows that my mother grew up in a house with dirt floors. No one knows that my father's parents were barely literate subsistence farmers.

The urgencies of betrayal and deceit are afoot in the world of 1939— the scourge of ideologies, Nazi genocide and Soviet executions. There's an implacable urge to kill. Thousands of people are already in concentration camps, millions more will soon be murdered, millions starved to death. Stalin will murder 60 million while in power, Hitler will murder 20 million. Why would a man and a woman want to have children as the cult of death is raging?

In the wakefulness of Donna's nightmarish dreamscape, she sees her mother reared on a Lithuanian estate they would flee to save their lives from Russian Soviet enemies. The communists carried lists of people to be executed—teachers, priests and professionals—to make room for the people's paradise. Her paternal grandfather is on the kill list. He's a globetrotting, bridge-building engineer. Her mother speaks five languages. Both of our mothers do. High levels of education are also reasons to put you to death. The kill lists are broad and comprehensive. Even owning two cows could have you listed as a bourgeoisie slated for death.

Many choose to fight the invaders, some collaborate to save their lives, most escape into their private worlds. Donna's father, rebelling against parental expectations, learns to play the organ, and dreams of a career in music as a concert pianist—Schubert, Chopin, Debussy, Rachmaninoff—he's seeking Franz Liszt piano virtuosity. Such hopes were shattered as marauding Nazis and Communists took turns murdering, starving and exiling the inhabitants of Eastern Europe.

Our parents were among the fortunate who survived the kill lists. They came to America, bearing us with them. In the years to come we would feel their loss in the plaintive songs they sang at social gatherings, and in the wistful words of the Lithuanian national anthem imploring God to protect the mostly rural nation from terrifying enemies. They lost their country, their professions, status and homes, but saved their lives, and ours, when they fled to the United States.

My mother, once an elegant woman of diplomatic postings, became a janitor at the Domino Sugar refinery on the East River in Brooklyn. Donna's father abandoned Schubert and Chopin to work as a factory hand in Philadelphia, skilled at chrome-plating the kitchen chairs that were sold with linoleum-topped tables of that era. He lined his shoes with cardboard to make them last longer so that he could buy new shoes for Donna and her brother. Her mother sewed garments in a sweatshop. You can call such self-sacrifice on behalf of children sentimental sweetness, you can call it hard-boiled domesticity, or you can also call it love. Call it what you will. A sense of entitlement is not among our inheritances. Shadows can follow us on sunless days, unseen fears stalk our Lithuanian woods. Our family histories echo loss, the ashes from burned fortunes and crushed dreams.

"You're going to catch a cold," Donna says.

Out in front of us, maritime activity has slowed for the night. Container ships carrying freight ply the waters of Puget Sound. Cruise ships head out to Victoria and Vancouver in British Columbia, and return. There are naval ships, fishing boats, and tugboats too. The ferries keep going, day and night.

It starts to drizzle. Neither one of us is ready to go inside. How did we manage? What's kept us together? There's much in a marriage that's repetitive, gone over dozens and dozens of times. Lovemaking, yes, also boredom, routine, children, diverse needs, illness, disappointments, rival attractions, compromises, and duties one had never anticipated.

Donna was fifteen and living in Philadelphia when we started dating. I was eighteen. A friend and I had gone to a winter camp near Drexel in Pennsylvania, organized to keep Lithuanian girls and boys safely in the ethnic fold. We were visiting an ice-skating rink nearby.

I saw her first. Her hair lushly dark, brown eyes quick and curious, her smile directed at someone else. "She's beautiful, isn't she?" my friend said. I tried to keep from looking at her. But every turn she made on the ice, and on the clattery wooden boards off the ice, I seemed to notice. She was bundled in a sweater and a jacket, and wore a tartan skirt and tights. Though the air was cool most of us were warm, and some of us were sweating from exertion. She wore figure skates, the blades notched at the front to dig into the ice on pirouettes. I preferred speed skates, long flat blades designed for velocity.

Lights glowed brightly across the ice. The PA system poured out sappy music. We went round and round the rink, like two planets not meant to meet. She glided smoothly to the concession stand, and pulled her cap off to adjust her shoulder-length hair. Several strands were weighed with ice crystals. She was too busy to notice me, tipping her head one way and then another to brush the ice away.

"You can say hello to her," my friend encouraged, then disappeared to find his own interest.

Conversation seemed impossible. Looking to pay for her Mars candy, she realized she'd left her wallet in the car. I overheard her explain this. She's too young to drive a car. The thought of a boyfriend driver in her life challenges my eagerness to know her. I push several coins across the counter to pay for her candy bar. The clerk takes my money without a glance.

"I'll pay you back," Donna says.

"It's okay. Don't bother. How's the Mars bar?"

She looks at the chocolate, caramel and nougat. "You want some?" She holds it up, and smiles. I take a bite. She takes a bite. I take a bite. Several more bites, and the Mars bar is gone. I ask her to skate with me. Bit by bit we find a few words to speak. I'm awkward with feeling, and can't concentrate on anything except her. I offer to teach her a couple ice skating tricks. She pretends not to know any.

We're no longer in the romantic moment of our teenage youth, parked near a bench, and Donna wondering, *is this guy going to kiss me or not?* Her eyebrows are still wide and dark and her eyelids slightly puffed after lovemaking. A tugboat is pulling a barge out on the Sound. The raindrops glisten on her cheeks, like tears falling on my heart.

Donna is petite. Five feet one and a half inches tall, a hundred and five pounds when we married. She remains self-possessed, self-directed, dark-haired, strong-willed, her eyes bright with expectation. She calls me her Twinkletoes, though I'm as graceful as an injured giraffe on a dance floor. Our two dogs she's named Nikki and Sophie, but more familiarly they're known as Mouse, a tiny Yorkshire Terrier, and Bozo, the cuddliest and possibly the dumbest Brussels Griffon on earth. Depending on the circumstances, either one may be called Twit.

"What?" she asks.

"I don't know if we should do the deal."

We listen to the chimes.

We can remain silent, companionable in our solitudes, secure in the knowledge that one or the other is near, even if potential disaster might be close. Her mother couldn't handle her; her father took the belt to her. She's the talkative one, always asking questions. She believes she's the silent one, and I'm the unreliable narrator.

Why are we out on the deck in the middle of the night, unable to sleep?

We've recently met a charming stranger who's proposing a risky business deal. I'm hearing the man's seventy-six trombones, a marching band I want to join. She hears the click-click sounds of a pair of dice that may come up snake eyes and bankrupt us.

We've made a life in America. Good luck and hard work both helped; our children are a gift. Yet our happiness can be provisional. You would think that the cable TV media narrators and the plentiful book gurus telling us how to live a passionate life and make a fortune—you would think they could actually *inform* your ability to live a life, write a book, or earn a fortune.

Keep on dreamin'.

One is left to leap into the fog alone.

There's no cavalry coming to rescue us. Whatever light we need to guide us, we must find within ourselves, our experiences, our history. There's never enough light, and no certainty either. We've learned not to believe in totalizing systems, in religious or cultural absolutes, or in perfection.

The breeze lifts off the Sound and silence returns to the chimes. Two cruise ships float on the water like lighted candles. A few raindrops falling are promising more rain.

"We don't have to do it," I agree.

2

CARS, FREEDOM, LIFE ON THE MOVE—DONNA HAD A LEARN-
er's permit at fifteen. I didn't have mine until seventeen. Her
father was urged to "Buy a Chevrolet and see the USA" and did.
Neither of my parents learned to drive a car. At one time my father had
a chauffeur, and in New York City we had subways.

I'm not a car guy, though a number of cars have addled my mind.
The first car I coveted was the slope-nosed, sleek-sided, 1953 Studebaker
owned by a customer who came to Sam's Luncheonette in Brooklyn,
where I worked the counter—from age fourteen, except for shelter and
food provided by my parents, I earned all of my own spending money.

Employment at Sam's offered several attractions. I could eat whatever I wanted—lox and cream cheese on a bagel was my first step away
from Lithuanian cuisine. And given our strained financial home circumstances, this was a big step up from the economy fare our family
income provided us at home.

The bulk of the luncheonette business, as the name clearly states,
came at lunch. It required four people to help. Sam and his wife and

a brother-in-law handled most of the heat. The hectic tempo changed in the late afternoon, and by six it became a neighborhood hangout. I was eighteen when Sam put me in charge of the evening shift, which I worked solo. Bedford-Stuyvesant wasn't a Norman Rockwell safe-harbor neighborhood. On slow nights the occasional dodgy person might wander in. Not surprisingly, I welcomed the cop on the beat whenever he dropped by for coffee or cigarettes. I liked it even more if he stayed, and sometimes he did.

My favorite nights to work were Fridays and Saturdays. The business was faster and the crowd much larger, friendly and safe. Men from a wider section of Brooklyn than my neighborhood gathered on those weekend nights to plan a soiree or discuss excursions upstate to Borscht Belt Catskill resorts, Grossinger's among them.

The regular gang didn't include women, although they were the objects of much male-centered planning. Many of the customers had lived in the neighborhood when they were younger, then prospered and moved out. The Studebaker owner was among them. He was the owner-manager of a "going concern," as the term was then used, a company that brokered wholesale food. The much-admired United States poet laureate Maxine Kumin recalls in her memoir *The Pawnbroker's Daughter* that her mother experienced extreme social shame on account of her husband's trade, described as that of a "broker" to imply a stockbroker instead of a pawnbroker. But shame of any kind, let alone shame about successful mercantile and merchant efforts, wasn't in evidence at Sam's. The men joyfully competed to be one up on each other. My boss, Sam Gershfeld, sweat staining his shirt, energy in his movements, remains in my memory as one of my favorite bosses.

Some say that the dream of opportunity, often described as the American Dream, is a delusion, others say it's propaganda that favors the already rich, others swear by its democratic hope, and still others decry its demonic work demands, and occasional lack of morals. None of that was visible to me in my youth. What was visible was the Studebaker. This zippy-looking car morphed into a symbol of self-employed success, and the urge to own one's own business became imbedded in the far corners of my mind. I would mix the Studebaker owner's egg cream with special diligence, happy to serve a man who could thrive without having to work for anyone else.

But I had no car the first year or so after I got my driver's license. The Greyhound bus became a miracle of timely efficiency in my dating plans. I could travel a hundred miles in roughly two hours from Brooklyn to Philadelphia to visit Donna. From those early days I've been a fan of public transportation. But who can deny an American kid his or her car? The carriage toward independence, adventure, free association, fun, girls, and sometimes trouble. American, rather than Lithuanian American, is how I defined myself.

But before I bought a used car, I borrowed one. Borrowed from kind adults willing to trust me. A Lithuanian pastor from Jersey City, as worldly as the more familiar Irish model, frequently visited his physician brother who shared a house he bought with my parents as partners, and on those visits that could last several days, the pastor, who liked me, lent me his car. The glistening blackness of his Oldsmobile 88 still shimmers in my memory. Driving it, I approach a crest in the road, accelerating flawlessly. The long, sleek ebony hood prods the sky, rides the crest in a leap, settles commandingly onto the road, and continues effortlessly—a celestial ride.

Sam's car, a Chrysler, the eponymous New Yorker, I liked more. He allowed me to borrow it on several occasions. The vehicle was showy and theatrical. The two-tone paint job was divided by saber-like chrome slashes. It had a bulky, glittery, Wurlitzer-styled dashboard and a passionately chrome-charged interior. The New Yorker was not only swashbuckling, and irreverent, it was cheerfully extravagant.

Eventually, I did buy a car affectionately remembered as a "beater." In fact I owned a string of beaters because they tended to fall apart unexpectedly. There was a funereal Hudson with slant windows and a backseat the size of a bedroom, then a perfectly normal Ford, as black as Henry Ford wanted. I owned a boxy, glossy, lemon-colored Plymouth that was stolen. But I was mostly in love with an old Buick Roadmaster with Dynaflow transmission. This might have been a sign of my youthful coarseness, a callow disregard for European cultural finesse, but I loved the memory of that Roadmaster most. Even the name was masterful. The leather upholstery was two-toned and the dry leather cracked; the steering wheel had a magnificently large horn ring. Wire-mesh covered chrome "ventiports" on the sides of the front fenders convinced me that the monster inline eight cylinder engine needed all the oxygen it could grab once I stepped on the accelerator, busting up the air in front of me with a roar on my way to see Donna.

This aging beast set me back a summer's wages. The exhaust had a deep-throated sound on account of a rusted muffler. I couldn't afford to replace it, but I liked it that way. These were the days before emission testing. The Roadmaster announced my presence in any neighborhood, mostly Donna's neighborhood.

3

CROSSING OVER FROM BROOKLYN TO MANHATTAN ON MY way to Jersey, I entered the Holland Tunnel. I dreaded the tunnel. Claustrophobia was one thing, also the strange fear that the tunnel might spring a leak and everyone inside the tunnel would drown. In those days of minimal ventilation, the air inside the tunnel raised the most alarming concerns: you could die breathing the stuff. The exhaust fumes were especially acrid that day and the Transit Authority cops walking the tunnel beat must have been punished to be working the tunnel, or maybe they were getting extra pay for hazardous work.

I closed the windows to breathe through my mouth—as if eating gasoline fumes was somehow healthier—and drove to Avon-by-the-Sea, where Donna worked that summer.

Despite the upper-crust name, Avon-by-the-Sea was a middle-class enclave where the not-so-rich traveled to feel the summer breezes they couldn't afford in the Hamptons, already copyrighted to privilege the rich. It was a good place, with many summer rentals and guesthouses that offered room and board by the week or month. Donna worked at one of these boarding houses, owned by a Ukrainian widow. It was an establishment famous for its African American cook, Odessa, the star of the place. Her presence alone was responsible for half the summer guests returning each season.

Donna's boss located every chit, addressed every smudge, every dust weevil, and had it itemized. The girls working housekeeping duties worked tirelessly, like shuttles on a loom. Some were saving for college, a distant dream. The reward for Donna was the free time she had to herself after four o'clock each afternoon. The other reward was Odessa's cooking, all you could eat.

There was something soft and lovely in the summer by the sea. The scrub and brush on the sides of the roads and the vanilla-scented pines and the feel of sand underfoot, all contributed to my good fortune to escape Brooklyn. The baby oil we smeared on our bodies and the lanolin creams on our faces kept our skins alert to the sun, and the touch of our hands—that was heaven, the feeling of youth.

If much of youth is reduced to its charming romantic poses and desperate dating angles, we enjoyed as much of those as we could. Often such passages are imprecise, vaguely hopeful, sometimes soulful. Our dreams were poorly informed as to life's uncertain prospects. We didn't have the leisure or money to look for a "lifestyle" to suit our future, and we were indifferent to discovering our "authentic selves." Whatever we had, we had. Whatever was missing remained unknown.

Our teen curiosity was centered on pop icons, James Dean, Natalie Wood, Elizabeth Taylor, Elvis Presley and Chuck Berry. Our tradition was ethnic, but our youthful tastes were eclectic. Only a subliminal hint of the Ramones, some blues and a touch of Muddy Waters, Miles Davis, lots of country music, lots of Frank Sinatra, and the ever-lovin' Beatles, Buddy Holly too, along with Bo Diddley, The Rolling Stones, a taste of The Clash, Ray Charles and James Brown. We also loved Paul Simon and Art Garfunkel, and Joan Baez and Marianne Faithfull, Bruce Springsteen and the unscripted, culture-changing, forever life-altering, Bob Dylan.

There's no pattern here. No grand plan. No fixed pole. The stars kept coming, David Bowie, Madonna, Lady Gaga, George Michael. Diversity is America. Homegrown and immigrant. Anyone can try, everyone should. We admired, listened to, and heeded the call. We were on our way to becoming American.

The musicians we loved, along with my later in life friend Billy Squier ("Rock Me Tonight, Stroke Me") inscribed a huge change for a boy who once attempted to play a Lawrence Welk-inspired accordion unsuccessfully.

Jack Kerouac's *On the Road* had been published. Donna bought me a copy. Considering that she was a girl who was defiant and dutiful—the nuns almost convinced her to join them, the Kerouac book was a gift of exalted rebellion—miles and centuries outside the ethnic immigrant expectations that had most Lithuanian immigrants nesting amid the safety of family and church.

"What am I supposed to do with this book?" I asked.

"You're supposed to read it."

I handled the book carefully, as though it might be dangerous. I didn't much like reading fiction then, my literary adventuring limited to Rudyard Kipling's *Kim*, a book soon to be dumped in the postcolonial dustbin. Besides, there was much too much to learn in nonfiction: plain stated rules, dos and don'ts, debits and credits, secrets to success, lists of many kinds, formulas for living and advancing, seven or ten things I could do better with myself, mostly mechanical how-to things. In addition I was working several jobs—at the post office as a temp helper and at Sam's Luncheonette—I didn't have much time for reading.

Though I loved visiting Donna we weren't sleeping together. I couldn't afford to rent a room when I stayed over at Avon-by-the-Sea. I slept in my car. Today, the West Coast town where we live would have me arrested for sleeping in my car. But when I got to Avon-by-the-Sea that day, I experienced a passage of exquisite escape. We walked along the boardwalk holding hands. We bought cotton candy, we watched taffy being pulled and bought some for ourselves. We kissed, which in the rigid social values of innocent immigrant youth at that time, sealed the deal between us. We kissed some more and hugged and squeezed. The sea breeze and the smell of Coppertone freshened our intense physicality. This was heaven, our lives unencumbered, vivid in painted spring colors.

I wasn't yet Donna's official fiancé, but I was on the gossip train toward becoming one, provided I could overcome her family's possessive love for their daughter.

"How about it?" I asked.

"What?"

"Us getting married?"

"I don't know."

"We don't have to know anything."

My proposal of marriage must be among the least romantic ever spoken. She had plenty of boys interested, and her mother had another suitor in mind. I was afraid of losing her.

"How are we going to manage?" Donna wondered.

Her practical question seemed to imply that she'd accepted my impractical proposal, and it turned out that way.

4

PREPARED FOR NOTHING, UNPREPARED FOR MOST EVERYTHING else, Donna and I announced our engagement. We were thrilled; our parents were not. Both sets of parents were loyalists to the cause of freeing Lithuania from the Russian Soviet occupation, but politically they were askew from each other. My father came from the Catholic wing of moral activists, Donna's parents, though Catholic, her father an organist at church, came from the nationalist strain of loyalists. Surface similarities aside, the contrast between them went much further than membership in different political factions. They were deeply hostile to each other on a personal, social level, carrying with them the prejudice of centuries.

In photographs, and there are many, my father is often shown socializing at public events with my mother. From appearances they are an influential couple, one might even call them a power couple. My mother the "it" woman of her time; my father the leader of several political groups, a diplomat who would rise to become the ultimate leader of the exile organization to free Lithuania. His achievements are beyond anything I would reach. They're also a political couple, cosmopolitan, attending to appearances, sensitive to how their private lives might play out in public. One photo shows my mother in front of a Tri-motor airplane wearing a sporty hat that Ingrid Bergman might have chosen. Both were indifferent to sports, which Donna's father loved. My mother would eventually become a librarian at the Metropolitan Museum of Art. Both were good looking, accomplished, and had found in each other something that each of them wanted. Yet my mother and father are possibly the most ill-fated and unhappily married couple I would come to know.

Our parents didn't fit the adorable conventions we learned from studying Dagwood and Blondie cartoons, or watching *Leave It to Beaver* and *The Adventures of Ozzie and Harriet*, or *I Love Lucy*.

Donna's father was an artist at heart, though a family man too, affectionate, loyal, active in the Lithuanian community hall as its president, and a trustworthy guide to its financial affairs. His social obligations kept him tethered to the Lithuanian community. Many routine maintenance needs at home he ignored. Choosing his leisure carefully, he preferred to listen to classical music. Perhaps he was also rebelling against his upbringing at the hands of a strict, efficient, celebrated, world-trotting engineer father who demanded total obedience, and in the case of children, total silence at the dinner table. At any rate, Donna's father rarely troubled himself to fix anything in their Philadelphia house, and given their modest income, rarely hired anyone to do what was left undone.

Donna's mother, a college graduate, reared on an estate served by many servants, developed a lifetime indifference toward cleaning. She spurned cleaning but loved cooking. Such cavalier attitudes toward the bourgeois conventions of housekeeping and cleanliness might have been the downfall of many families, tattered by fierce argument, resolved in sullen looks. But I never heard Donna's parents raise their voice in anger at each other. A warmth flooded my senses when I visited. I understood only later that it fell to Donna from the age of twelve to tidy up at home so that no friend or visiting neighbor would think badly of her parents. An anxiety over housekeeping that exists even today.

Along with my graduation from City College, I earned a 1-A from my draft board. (1-A was fighting man stuff.) Donna and I were eager to get on with our lives, so I asked my draft board to call me up early in order to complete my military service as soon as possible. An "early" call-up could take several months, even a year. I looked for a job in the meantime. An ad in the long-gone *Journal-American* described a career in sales that would let me earn what I'm worth. Who can argue with that? I took a straight commission job selling Collier's books door-to-door, hoping to earn enough money to visit Donna regularly.

My team leader heads a caravan of two cars loaded with neophyte salespeople like me. We're an attacking force, insurgents selling encyclopedias. No base salary, no draw, no benefits, and lots of free advice from the team leader.

Nearly all of us are broke.

Several weeks into the sales job, I haven't sold a set of books. The team leader isn't disappointed. I cost him the price of an otherwise empty seat in his car. A boisterous curly-haired man, he drives a glistening Cadillac with magnificent tail fins and two rocket-like rear lights attached to each one. He tells me it takes a while to get the hang of sales. Most of his recruits don't last more than a month—I'm getting close. He releases us to our work with a comment that the neighborhood "looks good."

It's a hot New York City day. Smudgy wet patches take the morning's starch out of my shirt. I climb the stairs of a building assigned to me. My

white collar is soiled with soot and sweat. One step, two steps, a stair-
case landing, two steps twice, one step, a landing—I'm rising in a Bronx
tenement building, public housing, low-income housing, "the projects."
Graffiti descends in a gentle spiral of bleakness on the solid wall. Two
steps twice, one step, a landing, five doors to the right I find 5A and ring
the bell. A young woman opens the door. I tell her I'm selling books for
her children. She smiles, surprised by my earnestness.

For every set of books I sell I earn a commission; my team leader
earns an override. The purchase price can run past a hundred dollars—a
fortune in those days—and always on credit. The sales company orga-
nizers, two teachers, receive another override on my effort. Perhaps
they think of themselves as freelance educators.

We're all leeches.

The customer, a brunette with deeply etched, shadowed brown eyes,
seems amused. She can't be much older than me. She had mailed a card to
our office inquiring about the books we were selling. That lead called me
to her door. I hold a plastic portfolio at my side, presenting myself as an
impresario of small things. She's pretty. I must seem all angles and tight-
fitting corners. Clearly a person she can handle with ease. She invites me
in. Her young son looks on curiously. The baby is sleeping.

A novice like me has to learn to move with authority. This counts
for a lot. The less authority I have, the more this counts: the flourish,
the telling gesture. The solid voice of indisputable weight and influence
also helps. Unfortunately, I have a questioning tone. I'm also six feet
and weigh only one hundred sixty pounds. This is not how the cringe-
inducing Henry VIII looked. I have to work harder to build a presence.
I need to absorb the space, have it stick to me, make it seem that there's
no place for the customer to go but nearer to me. In a flourish meant
to be authoritative, I drop my portfolio of posters onto the floor. The
woman looks at me sharply. "You just woke the baby."

There's only a slight whimper at first, and then the baby really starts to cry. Her older boy doesn't look happy either. My customer goes into the alcove near the kitchen and picks up the baby. Her older boy starts to fuss more. I do the only practical thing I can think of—I retrieve a rattle from the floor, rattle it, make a goofy face at the baby, and hope my cooing works. The older child is amused and wants more attention.

After unsnapping the vinyl-covered portfolio, I unfold a large lithographic poster and smooth the creased rectangles on the floor. The poster depicts wisdom contained in books, book upon book in gold binding. The prints are beautiful, as captivating as stained-glass church parables. The saturated lushness of the posters lying next to the tidy knocked-about furniture—a love seat and an armchair—strikes a contrasting note, a conversation between the lushness of knowledge and strained economic means, promising the customer all that's missing.

My customer seems to like the break in her routine. There are extras to sell—a shorter version, an atlas, a history set—and each is depicted in an equally impressive and colorful poster. I cover her bare floor in the promising life of all the books she will probably never read. For "two dimes a day," I say—that was the sales pitch—she can purchase a set of books on credit that could help her children achieve success as valedictorians and scholars, doctors and lawyers.

The baby drifts off to sleep. Her older boy sits quietly on her lap. My pitch remains awkward, clumsy canned words placed in my head by my trainer. What if her children are never going to read the books? Maybe they will look at the pictures on occasion? That aside, Donna and I have always been optimistic for other people, expecting them to live supremely happy, wonderfully active, often in love, and accomplish more than most have any chance of accomplishing.

My customer says yes, she wants her children to grow up smart. Her hair is voluminous, dreamy-tangled, barely combed. The TV set on a rickety metal-legged platform blinks silently at us. Whispers of hair cross her forehead and a haunting, eager look comes over her as she sets her boy on the floor and gets onto her knees. She runs a finger across a glossy poster. I reach for my order pad. But when I turn around with my pad, I see three or four glistening drops on the poster. She wipes a tear streaking her cheek.

"I can't afford it," she says.

"Not even at two dimes a day?" I ask.

We both seem to know this isn't going to fly. Owning a landline phone in those days was the strongest signal that your sale might get credit approval, but she doesn't have one. In the harsh speech of commissioned salespeople my customer went from a lay-down—an easy sale—to a deadbeat. The posters on her floor feel slick as I refold them. I thank her for her time and I head toward the door. I turn around and say, "There's a library not far away." She acknowledges me with a goodbye nod.

Outside I do a postmortem with my trainer. He had cautioned us to love our customers, but not too much. Pushing for closure, the signature on the dotted line, demands steely aggression. He tells me that I should have placed the poster upside down to build suspense and engage curiosity. That I should not have paid attention to her good looks. That I should have sounded more authoritative. After planting the right words, setting the proper mysterious mood, mimicking a page-turner, only then should I have flipped the poster right-side up, stunning the buyer with the cornucopia of Western knowledge.

Early on I'm dusted by the performance art we call commerce. I'm a seaman at the bow of an icebreaker named *Capitalism*, churning through oceans looking for profit. It's hard work. Impersonal work. I can't get the woman out of my head for a month. I wish I'd left her the glossy posters.

5

VIETNAM, ALREADY A TINDERBOX WITH A LIGHTED FUSE, WAS a subject that kept cropping up. Applying the romantic wages of youth, I mention to Donna that if I'm ordered to a war zone we should postpone our marriage. Unspoken between us was the possibility that I could be maimed or killed in Vietnam.

"I don't like that," she said.

"What?"

"I don't like the delay. If we want to marry, we'll marry."

"Dead or alive?"

"That's not what I mean."

I wanted to say I'm sorry that I made such a bad joke. But I said nothing.

Soon after we made these plans I quit my Collier's encyclopedia selling job, and moved to a fourth-floor walk-up room a block away from her parents' house. To support myself, I did a short stint as a door-to-door salesman for Gerber baby food. The most interesting thing I learned on the Gerber job I could have learned had I read *The Great Gatsby* early on. Desire, sex, marriage, lust, love, hope, run on parallel tracks on a route that doesn't necessarily lead to the same station. The handsome field director owned a love nest in the city and kept a mistress. I use the patriarchal term *mistress* instead of the more appropriate words I would use today—companion, lover, partner or friend—to show the limits of language that prevailed in that earlier era. My field director's wife and kids were in the suburbs; he loved them too. But he was also proud of his amatory extra-credit achievement. One afternoon he felt a powerful urge to share his success with me. He might have intended a cultural lesson to teach me the rewards of male-fought capitalism, or it might have been simply a case of braggadocio. At any rate, he asked me to his city place to relax after canvassing a neighborhood.

It was a stoop-front-porch row house, similar to the one Donna's parents owned. It had a full kitchen, washer and dryer. Donna's parents had worked years to save enough money for a down payment to buy a house with a mortgage. He had done it in a flash, and his girlfriend lived rent free. She was a fine-looking woman, crafted with exquisite care, adorable gestures, lovely voice. She had the eyes of a snow leopard, a narrow waist, and a long torso. Her hipbones marked vitality. She offered me a drink I declined. She looked at herself in a mirror, as if I had offended her. I could almost feel the field director's hands sliding the length of her sylphlike body.

Visiting his love nest was like taking a side trip to see how male money dominated. But his girlfriend wasn't selling herself just for the transactional value of money. She worked at Wanamaker's department store, and had her own money. They really were hot for each other. You could see it in their eyes and the gentle movements as they touched, seemingly by accident. A visit to Thomas Jefferson's Monticello, though beautifully built, was more disappointing than my view of the Gerber love nest.

The architect of our Declaration of Independence kept a beautiful sex-slave, Sally Hemings, an erotic setup rightfully condemned because she was Jefferson's prisoner.

I mention the Gerber affair to Donna.

"Would you take a mistress?" she wants to know.

"I'm crazy for you."

She plunges the needle a bit deeper. "Just like the other guys."

"I'm not *just* another guy. I asked you to marry me."

"But you liked his mistress?"

"She was gorgeous."

"To sleep with."

"You're putting words into my mouth I refuse to speak."

She turns away, and then coolly, "Guys and money, and fucking."

"I'm broke."

"But if you ever get the money like the field director?" She doesn't wait for me to answer. "You don't have to come to dinner tonight." She was still living with her parents. "I'm not sure I want to love you anymore."

"For god's *sake!*" I cried. "Don't do this to me."

"I need to trust you," she said, and then backtracked in small steps, speculating, maybe she does love me, and maybe she doesn't, anyway, who's in control of such things? Then she said it was okay to come to dinner. That skirmish settled, my salesmanship at Gerber foods was only slightly better than it was selling Collier encyclopedias. Close to a bust. I should mention that there weren't many job opportunities for an immigrant kid about to be drafted.

There are excellent men and women with noble motivation who join the military for lifelong careers. I admire them and I'm grateful. In the days of the draft many men joined the regulars, known as Regular Army

(RA all the way!) But most men set on civilian lives found the call-up inconvenient. For these men "US" was printed on their serial numbers and embossed on dog tags to distinguish them from RAs.

These were savagely anti-gay times, long before President Clinton's half-hearted "don't ask, don't tell" approach to keeping gay men and women in the service, and before the Supreme Court honored our humanity by declaring equal marriage rights for all. One of the more daring draft avoidance gambits was to declare yourself gay when you weren't. It required planning, rehearsal, makeup—a pale foundation, burgundy lipstick, lavender eye shadow, lids thickly painted, false eyelashes with several layers of mascara—and then more rehearsal, and if you could get it, a note from anyone in the medical field. A friend dabbed his cheeks with blush, curled his eyelashes to hold more mascara, expressed ambiguity of desire in his interview. Not surprisingly he dodged the draft.

Some men subject to the draft sought to amplify a physical weakness into a disability. Some found privileged civilian jobs designed to keep them at home and out of harm's way. Some fled to Canada. Some were conscientious objectors, who served honorably in uniform in noncombatant roles.

There are many ways to serve one's country, and being a warrior is only one way among many. But that aside, I hold in my heart special contempt, long nurtured, long festering, long unvoiced, for one type of draft dodger: The "shock-and-awe" adrenalin-fueled politician and government official, subject to the draft as I was, who sailed us through a sea of lies to rush us into the Iraq War. Many of these feckless individuals artfully avoided putting skin in the game when it was their turn to serve in Vietnam. Either they won rolling student deferments to keep them out of the military until the conflict ended or they wheedled a coveted spot in National Guard units whose members were legally draft exempt. The Guard units were not only deplorably trained at the time, which was added insurance that the units wouldn't be called to active duty, the units were also impossible to get into without political connections.

At any rate, a 1-A draft classification in those days made you nearly unemployable. Companies that portrayed themselves as violently patriotic refused to hire you, fearing that they'd be wasting their money training a short-term employee. For a guy like me with no money, few prospects, and no connections, this meant hustling in dead-end jobs that paid straight commission. It might not have been legal to ask you about your draft status, but every employer asked. If you told them that you were 1-A, you didn't get hired.

In an effort to leave Gerber foods I scored a second interview for a salaried job with a consumer finance company. My potential employer asked me to show him my draft card. I fumbled about as if looking for my Selective Service card. I told him I'd left it in another wallet at home, but it was okay to hire me. I said I was 4-F—claiming a mild congenital heart murmur, my brother's condition. "It's nothing. I can shovel snow," I said.

He laughed. I laughed, too. A mutual wink. He thought he'd met a successful draft dodger. He hired me and I found myself riding in his Plymouth to collect past-due consumer-financing accounts.

I study the collection list my boss has given me. The next call on our list had financed a couch. Her husband had taken off, and she was behind four months. My boss had filed a lien on the borrower's household goods from the get-go—this was standard practice then, part of the application paperwork—but he wants to jump ahead in the collection game, thus we're heading to knock on her door.

"Are we going to take back the woman's couch?" I ask, attempting a knowledgeable tone.

He glances at the sheet I'm holding. "Repo? No way, man," he says. "What the heck would we do with it?" I must look puzzled. He goes on, "It's a piece of crap, a rent-to-own deal. Can't be worth more than ten percent what she'd paid for it."

The furniture rent-to-own outfit and our company had established a symbiotic carnivore relationship chewing up consumers. The furniture outfit pounced and sold the woman her crap, and like scavenging hyenas, we, the finance company, were now chewing on the entrails. I feel like an undercover agent of modest good intentions witnessing unfairness.

Skillful in his collection effort, he had convinced the young borrower that she needed to invite her mother to our meeting on the pretext of having mother available for moral support. We pull up to a modest stoop house. Inside, the debtor's mother sits worriedly on the couch financed by the company. She's a little overweight, wears a print dress. Alongside is her slim daughter. The daughter's eyes are round with the fear of the dispossessed. Both women sit gingerly well forward. They look as if they expect us to cuff them and haul them off the couch and deposit them solidly in Eastern State Penitentiary nearby.

My manager talks about the dire consequences that may come about as a result of the unpaid chattel loan: repossession, bad credit, shades of Dickens, an allusion to landing in jail for committing fraud. Celebrity businessmen today proudly declare that they'd used the "laws of the land" to bankrupt companies because repaying their creditors was too onerous, but this is not what the two women know about the law. They probably don't know that Mark Twain went on the lecture circuit he hated in order to earn the money to pay debts that had already been discharged through personal bankruptcy. There's a great amount of fluidity in such moral matters. The poor are always told to honor their obligations, the rich hire lawyers to find loopholes.

I'm as poor as the woman. I'm catching on. It's not good to be poor. Economic authority is organized to take advantage of the powerless.

I've been at work only a month and already I'm hating my job. My manager has the friendly sweet patter of "good guys" blessed with the skill of winning concessions. He's so pleasant I would buy my Gerber foods from him. The women are plainly terrified, the mother more so: she's wringing her hands. Disloyal to the company cause, I sympathize with the women. The mother says she would like to help but doesn't have the money. My boss speaks cheerfully and asks if she'll "merely" cosign the note. Would she do this small favor for her daughter? The mother says yes, she'll cosign.

I'm too inexperienced to fully appreciate this coup. He has just notched another kill on his collection gun. Several signed forms later we leave the house. He's whistling softly, enjoying the success of his emotional duress on a warm summer day when the chestnut trees are in full leaf.

The months at work go fast and the day approaches for me to report for military service. I have to inform my boss that I had been drafted to serve in the US Army. I have to admit that I lied about my draft status. The philosopher who sheds much ethical light on our middle-class values, Immanuel Kant, would certainly disapprove of my deception, but since I was working for a company that cut a few moral corners I expected my boss to cut me some slack. Unfortunately, there wasn't much "thank you for your service" in those days. He called me a cheap-assed lying kid and threw me out the same day.

6

SO, IT TURNS OUT, I WAS ONCE A WARRIOR, THOUGH OF A rather tame kind. After winning my sharpshooter's badge on the firing range at Fort Dix, I found myself at Fort Gordon, near Augusta, Georgia, home of The One, the Godfather of Soul, James Brown. I'm completing advanced Signal Corps training. The Army had given me a form to fill out to indicate my preferred overseas postings. I listed Europe first, Latin America next. No one in a draftee's state of mind wanted to serve in Vietnam. The Army ordered me to the 33rd Signal Battalion, stationed at Fort Richardson, Alaska. I phoned Donna.

"We're getting married!"

That's what we planned, that's what we hoped for, desired, yet it seemed to surprise even us. Donna was too young to marry. She hadn't finished college. I was untested, untried, inexperienced except for a few low-level jobs, and without a clue how we were going to get by financially.

That year we were coming off of an extremely busy summer: my training at Fort Dix and then Fort Gordon, Donna attending college,

teaching at a Lithuanian Saturday school, and at a Jewish youth camp—
she was hired by the community responsible for Frank Lloyd Wright's
synagogue, as one of two Gentile camp counselors.

There were no such things as "bachelor" or "bachelorette" parties for
immigrant youth getting married. Instead, Donna and I agreed that she
should take a break and enjoy a few late summer days at a Lithuanian
summer camp for young adults on the shore of Lake Superior.

Unknown to us, a sinister storm was brewing.

Family emotions, as most everyone comes to understand soon
enough, are explosive. The poet Philip Larkin declared: "They fuck you
up, your mum and dad." And sometimes they do. My mother favored
me, my father would disinherit me. But neither one wanted our marriage to go forward. They knew they couldn't change our minds, so they
intrigued behind our backs to kill our engagement. The intended execu-
tion came in the form of a letter from the person I trusted supremely,
plotting along with my parents. Claiming to be a witness at the camp
Donna had attended, the letter writer condemned her as mischievous,
childlike, joyfully crass, and possibly unfaithful.

Othello raged in my blood.

Donna is attractive, sensual, appealing, vital, and irrepressible—as
beautiful as Elizabeth Taylor was at age nineteen in the film *A Place in
the Sun*. What guy wouldn't want her? A platoon of potential boyfriends
had courted her. One of them was the son of an Italian American auto
dealer, his future assured, another was a rising young sales executive
at Nabisco, a brand manager. Young men with better prospects than I
could command as a private in the US Army.

I ate the poison fed to me—I couldn't win this beautiful girl. A prize
beyond my reach. My self-doubt rocketed, emotional afterburners
glowing.

As a platoon squad leader, I was helping a chubby draftee dismantle and clean his M-1. We didn't want to get the staff sergeant on the wrong side of us. We repeated the effort to break down and reassemble the M-1 over and over.

"Jesus," he said. "What's going on?"

"What?"

"What the fuck is the matter with you?"

"Nothing is the matter with me."

"Your hands are shaking."

"No they're not." I gripped the stock of the M-1.

"You're fuckin' shaking."

This was the beginning of the end. I knew it. Donna must know it. We were barely into our teens when we first met. What we couldn't learn about men and women from observing them, we learned from each other, not the best teachers. What could we have known so early in our lives?

Reading literature could have helped. As Virginia Woolf says so well, "To read a novel is a difficult and complex art." The reader gets to witness a character's moral virtues and faults—greed, hate, love, envy, loyalty, also ignorance, arrogance, bullshit, blindness and betrayals. By revealing such in the people we meet on the page, literature offers an alternative course of life study, insight into human schemes, desires, fantasies and frailties. But as I had mentioned already, I didn't read much literature then, not enough anyway.

Thoughts of vengeance pursued me.

I didn't recognize the complex interplay of emotions below our surface rationality. The letter writer held a grudge against Donna, disliked her, perhaps hated her. My shabby reading habits hadn't prepared me to face what I had not seen before in my life: intimate family malice, calculated harm, a plot, my parents persuading a person I trusted to send me a poisoned letter.

I broke our engagement.

Donna kept my letter. I've re-read it recently, a heartless letter, a cruel letter, blind and bitter, and foolishly young, a letter that decades later fills me with anguish. What ignorance drove me? How to explain it? I'm not typically undisciplined, or gullible, but I can be impulsive, and I was all those three things at once.

Her father, a proud man, told Donna to dump me. "Good riddance." But her willfulness was as strong as mine. She flew to Fort Gordon, Georgia, on a DC-3 (yes, on a DC-3) to confront the lies.

The winds were blowing that hurricane season, gales winding up from Florida. The beaches were pummeled, the pines whipped for mercy's sake. She was slender and suntanned. Her hair fell to her shoulders. She had a narrow waist and delicately shaped wrists and ankles. We were holding on, barely holding on to each other. The air was muggy, damp and adhesive. I told her what I'd been told by the person I'd trusted supremely. She laughed, and then turned angry. "How could you have thought that of me? Wasn't I more than a mere girl to you?"

"This will haunt me."

"Those lies, those lies! Couldn't you see past them?"

"I can't stop thinking about you."

"You've no right to be so unkind to me."

"I love you still."

"What is it like? This useless love of yours?"

Her question was a shadow on my heart. "I didn't mean it that way."

"You're not gentle."

"I'm just a guy. I don't want to be rough."

"But you've stabbed your own heart by abandoning me."

"Don't look at me that way. I'm not deranged."

"I've given you my soul. I don't want to live without my soul."

The light caught her fine neck, forehead and high cheeks, a dimple on the right one. Her beautiful skin and lustrous brown hair glowed. Her eyes observed life intensely.

Fort Gordon is near Augusta, part of the South known as Georgialina. James Brown, The Godfather of Soul, is its famous citizen. We stopped at a chitlin' eatery that had a jukebox. A man and a woman took turns feeding it coins.

James Brown sang, Try Me.

My military buzzcut made me look very young. Donna looked even younger. We shared a plate of green fried tomatoes.

"I need you," I said.

"For how long?"

She knew I had done her wrong. She'd flown to Augusta, but she wasn't sure what she'll do. Will she stay with me, will she break with me. The couple feeding the jukebox started to dance. Several more customers entered the place. James Brown sang, "Walk with me; Talk with me." I repeated his words.

"You can't carry a tune," Donna said.

"I wasn't singing."

I finished my beer and we got up to dance. We didn't leave the dance floor for several more dances. I paid my bill. As we were heading out the door James Brown was singing, Please, Please, Please.

We booked a motel and didn't sleep that night. Darkness lingered on restless earth. Skin-to-skin we tore out our hearts and laid them side-by-side. At dawn, in the shining hope of another day, we renounced our dependence on anyone other than us, and renewed our vow to marry.

Neither of us had money, and none was now forthcoming from the usual parental sources. "I'm not afraid to be poor," Donna said. We scrounged up enough money to eat breakfast at Howard Johnson's.

"But I don't want to be poor," I said.

"I'm not afraid."

"I hate being poor."

"We can be poor together."

"You're a dreamer. People will take advantage of you."

"Not if we're married."

"But you just told me that—"

She placed a finger over my lips to indicate silence. We had much to think about. As financial family orphans, we planned to elope and save our parents the expense and the irritation of seeing us married against their wishes. We were looking for legitimacy, rules and regulations—but who are the authorities? If we can't trust our parents, who else could we trust? Why trust anyone? Outside our happiness to marry, our worldview darkened. We began to see a universe in which no one could be trusted, or relied on, at least not for long.

In a last-ditch effort to stop our marriage the leader of the Lithuanian community in Philadelphia, guided by my father's social and diplomatic aura, showed up at Donna's house to demand an end to our engagement. Donna felt humiliated by his visit. It foretold of her expulsion from the community, a kind of exorcism, a kind of condemnation. She leapt up from her seat in the family living room she could no longer think of as her own, and told her parents they could now live without her.

Immediately afterward an explosive new rumor titillated the immigrant community with the news that Donna was pregnant, and we were trying to make it legit. (A false rumor. But a scarlet letter nonetheless.)

What did we need for a marriage license? Not our parents' permission. Several Army buddies helped finance our romantic adventure by "contributing" roughly $300 to poker pots I won. We were ready to roll off on our own—elope—when her parents, to save their own honor in the eyes of the immigrant community, offered a concession to our willfulness. They agreed to pay for the expense of a reception to stop us from eloping. I kept the invoice from D.F. McCallister & Sons Caterers, Philadelphia, and the use of the Gold Room for sixty-five guests: $303.58.

Donna borrowed a friend's wedding dress and I, a private in the Army, chose to be married wearing my enlisted man's uniform. Our wedding rings, including a marquis-cut diamond engagement solitaire, set us back $315. (I sold the Roadmaster.) We were married at Saint Andrew's, a Lithuanian parish church. Her dowry was $0; my principalities amounted to $0; our assets unknown. It was December 1963, a year wreathed in tragic national events.

A month prior, President John F. Kennedy was shot. I was on the parade ground at Fort Gordon when I heard the terrible news. Sadness washed across America. Hearts were stilled. The bars went empty. National cohesion and like-minded thinking pivoted in that year.

That year *The Beverly Hillbillies* had more than one-third of Americans watching it on TV. The long-running *Adventures of Ozzie and Harriet* was still going strong. *The Donna Reed Show* was a hit, and *Perry Mason* kept us guessing until he solved the crime. Everyone, it seemed, got married, and wanted to get married. Divorce was rare. Girls were shamed into giving up babies born outside marriage; boys were praised for "being boys." Crime was satisfyingly punished. Mothers stayed at home, and husbands "brought home the bacon."

The Production Code of the Motion Picture Association of America was working hard to sell us a sanitized, homogenized, and false version of "the American Way" (white, church-going, gender-defined, unthinkingly racist). Though a film based on Vladimir Nabokov's *Lolita* had squeaked by with Code approval, and several pictures were released without Code approval, the uplifting naïveté of the Code banned much of human experience from the screen, along with profanity stronger than *damn* or *hell*.

But the culture was changing. In hindsight we can see how the changes would lead to our culture wars today.

LSD was then legal. Marianne Faithfull, singer, songwriter, Mick Jagger's lover, called LSD "Fantastic!" Betty Friedan fired her salvo across complacent gender borders with *The Feminine Mystique* in the year we were married. Bob Dylan's "Blowin' in the Wind," "A Hard Rain's A-Gonna Fall," and "Don't Think Twice, It's All Right," were also released in 1963. Freedom Summer arrived the following year. Volunteers descended on the South to register voters. Rachel Carson got the environmental movement under way with her book *Silent Spring* a year earlier. Ralph Nader launched consumer advocacy with a piece in *The Nation* that led to *Unsafe at Any Speed*. The pill was approved for contraception a few years earlier and had become a big hit. Amid these cultural winds and exciting changes we set out on our married life.

My parents, though unhappy, came to the wedding and the reception. The menu included fresh fruit cup, soup, a potato croquette and roast young turkey with English filling.

My brother-in-law loaned us his car for a honeymoon in the Poconos. All of this activity was squeezed into the space of a few weeks before I reported for duty in Alaska. Donna joined me soon after, where we lived off base near Fort Richardson, and she worked at a bank in Anchorage.

As with many men drafted and tumbled together in the armed forces, I felt a life-changing engagement with the diversity and otherness of people. Several commanding officers arranged time-in-grade waivers to speed my promotions through the enlisted ranks. I was even urged to attend Officer Candidate School, all to no avail. I was in a rush to get on with our civilian life.

Before I was discharged from active service my father died of a heart attack. Donna took my hand on hearing the news. I pulled away, she let my hand drop. We stared at each other. "He never loved me," I said.

"Don't feel guilty."

"He's my father."

"You're not to blame."

We were still broke. She remained in Anchorage and I borrowed money from a serviceman's aid society for a flight home. I arrived just in time to be helpful to my mother.

7

THE PLACE OF MEN IN OUR WORLD HAS BEEN MUCH DIS-
cussed, analyzed, deconstructed, and written about. With clon-
ing and asexual forms of reproduction now available, advanced
possibilities have been proposed to free the world from men, a world
made more secure for women: There would be no rape, no murder, and
no war, and possibly no pornography, though that last is suspect. At any
rate, the need for men and their testosterone-fueled judgment is under
critical analysis as never before.

Setting aside the mutability of gender, men resist easy simplification. My father was a country boy. His older brother rose to become
the chief banking officer in Lithuania before the Soviets invaded. He
paid for my father's PhD in France, where my father polished his country manners into well-bred decorum, and a diplomat's aura. He never
failed to dress impeccably afterward. He wore stylish tortoiseshell eye-
glasses. His high forehead dominated his cautiously gray-blue eyes. A
bow tie set up a long neck.

I need to remember my father's barely literate beginnings. Did he tend to the sheep, the cows? Did he help his father behind the plow? I need to remember the energy and ambition and the talent required to go beyond his station at birth as the child of subsistence farmers. I need to remember, too, my mother's childhood house with the dirt floors in every room except one. Her father prospered as a man who hired women to weave carpets, sold to the rising bourgeoisie. The power and water that his operations required was provided by a windmill, from which he would fall to his death in his seventies.

Donna and I visited our parents' Lithuanian homes. We saw the well in the front yard from which my mother drew water, and in Donna's case the long lost grand estate, where household staff once roamed to serve Donna's grandparents and mother. These journeys into the past offered several revelations, some not visible in photographs our parents left us.

The cruel passions of conquest reached hurricane force in the days before World War II. My mother and father had a four-year-old son—my brother—and my mother was pregnant with me. In that time and place, I must have been the most unwelcome unborn burden a woman could bear. Could that explain a lifetime of melancholy, hers and mine?

Why would my competent father want to abandon the safety of his posting in neutral Sweden to take a post that would endanger the health of his pregnant wife and unborn child? Was it ambition? Service to the nation? Did my mother encourage him? Or did the job of first counsel in Sweden chafe at his ambition? Perhaps he desperately wanted to become an ambassador? Why else would he take the promotion as the *chargé d'affaires* in Poland—in charge as an ambassador, but not yet the ambassador.

A short time after my father's new posting, Hitler attacked Poland and Stalin demanded Lithuania's surrender. The two dictators had signed-off on a twisted, secret, sinister conspiracy to split and occupy eastern Europe. They started WWII as allies. Lithuanians and their nation became history's pawns.

My parents fled Poland by train. Traveling light, my mother must have insisted that they take the engraved silver box commemorating my father's Swedish diplomatic service, a gift etched with the signatures of his diplomatic colleagues. I'll become the keeper of this rare historical gift containing so many memories, and the sadness of lives bravely lived.

It's unclear if Hitler's blitzkrieg dive-bombers, or his Soviet allies, bombed and derailed the train. Probably Russian operatives flowing into Lithuania. My brother, mother and father survived the tangle of smashed cars upended. My mother was rushed to a hospital in Kaunas where she gave birth to me. In an odd coincidence of history, three years later, in February, one of the worst months in World War II, on the same day that The Rolling Stone's founding band member, Brian Jones, was born in England, Donna's mother delivered Donna in Kaunas, Lithuania.

In time, my father would become the president of the effort to free Lithuania from Soviet occupation. His card described him: Dr. A. TRIMAKAS, Professor, President of the Supreme Committee for the Liberation of Lithuania. A powerful achievement, a grand, courageous effort. A wonderful cause. The position offered what some would consider a gratuity as salary. Our family survived on his pay from itinerant teaching gigs and my mother's janitorial labor.

He wasn't one to offer praise—I doubt he received any praise himself working on the farm, perhaps not a stitch, not a word, not a single "I love you." So it startled me to find a card in my mother's treasure box, a card on which he had written *Valio Jada!* (Bravo Jada!) Praising my mother, addressing her with my mother's familiar name. Why did he praise her? How did she win his respect? Arrange an event? Influence some political matter? In one of the stories that settle in a child's mind,

I recall her saying she had saved my father's life during wartime by bribing a train conductor with a pound of lard to allow my father to board a train that would take them to safety. With so much at stake, with so much in the past, would any man today write such a formal salutation to his wife of many years and many trials? My mother kept this card. Perhaps the only praise she ever received from him. I'm left to wonder where were the hugs, the kisses?

So many questions; so few answers.

My father's accomplishments were many and varied—he served good people and good causes faithfully, a man you could trust. Yet one sad day he confessed to me that he'd wished for a career in the theater, perhaps a dramaturge, maybe an actor, or a producer, maybe a playwright. I don't know what to make of it now, how to deal with the past. This I know: he wanted to get off the farm, and did.

The requiem Catholic High Mass my mother arranged for my father's funeral was awesome to witness—choreographed with a monsignor and two priests in a synchronized ballet on the marble steps leading toward a gold tabernacle set on an altar blazing with Rococo gold that reached toward the ceiling. The sacred music performed—I don't recall if it was some portion of Mozart's Requiem that my father loved, or perhaps it was Chopin's funeral march—the music felt ethereal, indeed heavenly.

My mother felt my father's death deeply, and felt guilty. Prior to his death she'd taken a lover. But even if she'd given her heart to another man, a portion of that heart remained eternally and faithfully in my father's possession. Troubled by the location of his grave that she had chosen under pressure of his sudden death, she had him moved to a more congenial pastoral site in a section hopefully named Resurrection. The new site had room for her, where she rests today.

What was most memorable to me about the events surrounding my father's funeral wasn't the large group of mourners at church and at the luncheon we had arranged, not the long line of cars escorted by motor-cycle cops heading toward St. Charles Cemetery on Long Island, or *The New York Times* staff-written obituary. What I remember most was that my brother—the firstborn, my father's favorite, the boy who became a Roman Catholic priest because my father desired it—did not come to the funeral.

I couldn't imagine what harm or urgency had detained my brother in Mexico to prevent him from coming. The international phone service at the time was sketchy. He didn't have a private phone line. We still used telegrams. My mother, stoic, refused to comment on his absence. It was only after her death when I became an executor of her paltry estate that I found a telegram to her from my brother. She saved it. Worried over it. Kept it. The telegraph was torn, smudged, wrinkled. I could feel her despair in that scrap of yellowing paper. I suspect she'd read it a dozen times, disbelieving, uncomprehending. Her eldest, her firstborn child, the one kept safe through murderous times during WWII, the son her husband dearly wanted, the youth for whom they had scrimped to pay for his private schooling and college tuition, the man for whom she had bought his first gold-plated chalice so he could turn wine into the Lord's blood at Communion, my brother, had informed his mother that he was too busy in Mexico with his priestly duties to come to my father's funeral. He promised to make up for his absence by dedicating a forty-eight-page pamphlet he was writing about the Blessed Virgin Mary to my father's memory—a reading pleasure that father and firstborn must now continue in the hereafter.

8

AFTER MY HONORABLE DISCHARGE FROM ACTIVE MILITARY service at Fort Lewis, Washington, Donna and I careened toward a fast-changing workaday world without a clue as to what we could do, or what might come next. We moved to Philadelphia so she could complete her college education and earn a BS in teaching at Temple University.

Big Steel hired me. The company was Dickensian. Its buildings housed inventory and machinery to cut and shape metal coils, bars and plates, before shipping them to customers. The glass-paneled roof of the main building had a number of panels missing, but the old building, enormous, stretched the length of a city block and housed a crane suspended on rails. The building wasn't the only thing old. The men were getting old working there. The cars they owned and parked in the employee parking lot tended to be new, the stock symbols of successful working-class toil—ultra-clean vehicles, some with four-on-the-floor (stick shift, four-wheel drive), glistening at night under the dim parking-lot lights. To finance these automobiles, the men slit steel coil, cut aluminum plate, and bent metal rods.

I worked the swing shift and Donna, who attended school during the day, studied at night. We had moved to an apartment in Germantown, a section of Philadelphia where Maxine Kumin grew up in a much finer house. There was a backyard we could use, but we avoided it. Our next-door neighbor was Lady Macbeth. She never spoke but would come out in the evening, every evening, to sharpen what looked to be the same butcher knife. I didn't like leaving Donna alone in the evening. For protection she had our Irish Setter. The dog loved everyone.

At work I'm in charge of getting the trucks loaded. One night the plant manager who had hired me to work as a line foreman shows up unexpectedly and stations himself in his air-conditioned, glassed-in office overlooking the plant's loading areas. His evening surveillance gives me a chill. So much of management is surveillance of people to enforce profit. Today it is electronic surveillance, digital spying, e-mail checking, phone tapping, smartphone tracking, computer keystroke tracking, voice recorders, and the traditional camera and shotgun audio surveillance. There's something totalizing, something dehumanizing, something prison-like and poisonous in this Orwellian surveillance.

I signal to a truck driver to move up the line. An empty truck and trailer drives into his loading position. The exhaust fumes are as bad as anything I'd smelled going through the Holland Tunnel. The crane operator lowers a hook from above, the loader straps the load, and the crane operator lifts it onto the truck's flatbed. A broken line of trucks stretches out into the night. All of them waiting to get loaded and get the hell on their way.

They're mostly gypsy drivers tonight. Non-union independent con-tractors eager to pick up a road-busting load and drop it off somewhere on the Eastern seaboard, perhaps in New Hope or Baltimore the next morning. The *slam crump whoomp* from a metal-bending press makes it hard to hear what one driver is saying. He appears to be annoyed with me. He rolls his eyes. Speeded-up loading and steel work don't go well together. An accident could easily pierce the men's leather-palmed gloves and steel-tipped shoes. The loaders know this, the crane operator knows it. The drivers don't care. They want me to rush their loading, speed up the crane operator, and hurry the come-along guys snatching loads. They want to *hit the road, Jack, and never come back no more, no more.*

I ignore the man's scorn. A worker secures a canvas cover with belaying pins. I signal the line to move forward. Brakes chutter and wheeze. Trucks stretching from inside the building and out into the night rev up.

There isn't a person punching a clock that night who doesn't know that my boss has come up from Mainline to stand behind the louvered window to watch and to judge how well I'm working the swing shift. He doesn't want to regret having hired me, but he must have some doubt, some suspicion that he's made a mistake.

The shift foreman returns from his break. We share a private moment as the line of trucks starts to move. Foremen in civilian life are what non-commissioned officers are in the military. We move the trucks. We get the work done and we're closer to the men than to the officers. We're expected to spend time with the troops, understand them. We're also expected to understand officers. The first thing we learn to understand about officers is that there are things officers don't want to know. So we might on occasion wink at goings-on that would be intolerable if exposed to management.

"What do the men say?" I ask the lead foreman. I'm not sure I fully understand the social part of my foreman job. My voice suggests that I'm ready to hear the good along with the bad. "Maybe I should do the shack?" I ask.

On one side of the Big Steel fabricating complex is a shack that's sometimes used as a speakeasy during the swing and graveyard shifts. Everyone at Big Steel had to know that a bottle was handy for a drink, even though heavy metal and booze go together no better than drinking and driving. In those more lax times the shack offered neutral ground where first-line supervisors such as myself could unofficially mix with the men. I had avoided the shack. I wanted to jump-start a management career. A reputation for being too close to the men on the line wasn't necessarily helpful. Besides, I was too much of a stick-in-the-mud. My undergraduate degree in science and architecture didn't prepare me for this. It was a good time to test a change in my management style.

I make my way past the steel storage areas to the shack. Metal sheeting covers the roof, and the noise inside is somewhat clattery. The stale smell of beer catches my attention, but I find no one there. I light up a cigarette. The moon illuminates the grounds, making a strange arrangement of silhouettes. There are several trees bordering one side of the shack, and there are railroad tracks next to the huge building housing the crane.

"Sleeping solo?" a man speaks up.

Startled, I look up at one of the trees. "What the hell are you doing up there?"

A man is sitting in the crotch of the tree. It's hard to see him clearly. He moves a little and the moonlight shines on him. I'm thinking of a character out of Washington Irving's "The Legend of Sleepy Hollow," uncertain if the Headless Horseman is going to appear next.

But not a horseman. I recognize the man in the tree as Serge. He's a small, compact man, but oddly, he looks disproportionately large in the tree. He's wearing a scoop-neck T-shirt that sags low at the neck and reveals muscle made taut from hard labor. There's something in his agile attitude that he shares with many middle-aged men in a losing battle to stay young.

"Had a fight with the old lady," he explains. (This was the era when wives, no matter how young and beautiful, were called "old ladies.")

"Get out of the *fucking* tree," I say.

Serge swings himself clumsily on a stout gnarled branch and shimmies up three or four feet surprisingly well before slipping into another tree crotch. "She doesn't want to sleep with me anymore. It's my shift that's killing us. She says I smell bad and my hands are raw."

At the end of the shift the men pull off their oil-stained gloves and head to the washroom to clean up. Metal filings can get under the skin even when you wear gloves. They have to use grease-dissolver first, which tends to be gentler than the gritty industrial soap if you've caught metal filings. Once the splinters are out, then they can use the industrial soap.

"Knock it off and get inside," I say. "Knock it off" was a vernacular improvement over "get out of the *fucking* tree." But he's not listening to me.

Not knowing what else to do, I leave him in the tree and get back to the plant to load trucks. Steel I-beams lie near, the smaller bays are filled with aluminum and magnesium bars, and the metal racks hold other alloys poured into bricks. The coil slitter's steel slitting noise makes me edgy. The start of each cut is like a knife being honed. Several hours into my shift, a steelworker comes over to tell me that Serge isn't back on the line. He says there's something strange going on with him in the men's bathroom. I go to check. I get past the swinging doors and at first I see nothing wrong at the industrial sinks where six men can wash up at the same time. The oil smell and the coolant smell permeates the air. I walk the line of partitioned toilets and, at the second-to-the-last partition, see the knees of a man kneeling in front of the toilet. I tap on the door and push it open. The sight of Serge with his head in the bowl repels me. I shut the door. "You sick?" I ask.

"No, no, no, no, no, no," he wails.

"Get your head out of the fucking bowl," I yell.

"No, no, no, no." His tone changes to a whimper.

The greasy warehouse air and the metallic odors make breathing difficult. The coil slitter rips and shoots a harsh peeling sound as I head for the plant manager's office. I feel as if we're all on the banks of a vast muddy river. It's wide and slow, but it's a powerful commercial profit-making river that no one can stop. Serge works the banks of this river as I do. In theory every man and woman is free to quit or to stay with a job, and that was true for me. But for most of the men that I met at Big Steel, they were free to work and eat or quit and go hungry. I was young and eager to try many things, but I see now that it wasn't skill or talent that made me optimistic—it was my youth.

The plant manager stands watch at the louvered office window as I approach. I imagine him thinking he's done too much impulsive hiring of late, the finger-to-the-nose and seat-of-the-pants and gut-feeling hiring that has something vaguely hopeful about it. He'd mentioned, jokingly, that I think too much. Controlling thought is a big issue for bosses and nations alike. Thinking tends to question the status quo, slows things down, offers challenges, interferences, confrontations, disrupting established ways.

Thoughts also tend to run free, jogging and observing, hopping about like jackrabbits, running like roadrunners, sometimes just running away. The plant manager motions for me to enter. His white shirt makes a light beam of his presence. I describe what's happened, a man's abject loss of dignity. "Serge is going to maim himself or kill himself. He thinks he's being unmanned."

"Emasculated," my boss says, letting me know who has the better vocabulary.

"Right," I say. "Can we switch his shift to days temporarily?"

"The man has to take responsibility for himself."

"He's smashed himself sick."

"That's not my problem. I've got a plant to run."

My boss is righteous, perhaps even pious. He rails against paying taxes to fix public roads but he orders overweight trucks out on the road. For him the moral logic is perfect. You can piss in the public commons to save yourself money as long as you keep your own house clean.

Capitalism has been reconfigured more than once, rearranged several times, dusted and polished. American individualism mated with capitalism has never been a docile combination. I know next to nothing about these larger ideas. I'm a grunt working the line, groping my way toward an understanding of the business culture. I'm also getting a practical education—how profit is fought for in the trenches. Some of the lessons go over my head, some are spurned, the details waver, but the memory remains.

9

BUT I LEFT YOU, DEAR READER, A WHILE BACK WITH DONNA and me standing out in the rain on the deck of our house near Seattle and us agreeing that "We don't have to do it." We've been asked to bet everything we own in a gamble that would have us borrowing a mountain of money to build a car palace for a man from Walla Walla.

"I wouldn't do it," our banker says, emphatic, urging us to pass on the risky one shot, all-or-nothing bet. "It's going to bankrupt you."

By the time we face this decision we've made a number of changes in our lives since our youth in Brooklyn and Philadelphia, and the completion of my US Army tour in Alaska. Donna had earned her teaching degree at Temple University, taught at an inner-city Philadelphia school and then at a suburban one near Seattle. Along the way we had launched several business startup possibilities, worked them, sold them and launched something new, a printing store that Donna is managing while I attempt to write a novel.

Among our jauntier efforts to break away from the laboring life, we looked into buying vacant land—"dirt," as slick real-estate operators tend to call it. In our case, 2.19 acres on Highway 99, an amount too small for a ranch, or an estate, but okay for a farm-outlet store or a small motel. Vladimir Nabokov, had he come to Washington state, would have immediately recognized the roadside location as a piece of the American experience, congenial to his imagination as he prepared to write *Lolita*.

The allure of commercial property ownership can infect even the most progressive and democratic. One imagines living like royalty collecting rents. One doesn't imagine the middlemen, the city inspections, the building code, the repairs, the leasing details, the fire marshal, the zoning requirements, or the rent checks returned that are stamped "insufficient funds."

Joan Didion was at *Vogue* when she took a correspondence course, a University of California Extension class in "shopping center theory" that featured Northgate Mall in Seattle, one of the first malls in the nation. Didion had fallen into an unprofitable habit of writing fiction, she says, and she thought that a few shopping centers might support that habit "less taxingly than a pale-blue office at *Vogue*."

Highway 99, though unheralded in pop culture, was once a collection of wagon trails in the nineteenth century that helped westward-ho pioneers and other seekers of fortune to travel up and down the West Coast. The trails were eventually connected and paved to make travel easier. Around the time Henry Ford made cars affordable and the gold bugs had given up their pans and shovels, real-estate speculators proliferated like tadpoles, hoping that the next intersection might become a profitable land boomlet serving motels, shacks, fruit stands and cabins along the highway. Post-World War II drivers started buying cars in unprecedented numbers and President Eisenhower ushered in the grand expansion of the highway system.

Portions of Highway 99 had to be buried under the newer interstate system, but much of it survived, serving small towns as their main north-south highway parallel to Interstate 5.

Donna and I were in our early thirties, no longer naïve but not especially wily either. The seller of the land, a long-time real-estate investor, was willing to finance. He had been trying to unload the land for years, and no one was buying. A buyer's market. Donna and I looked at it, and not knowing any better, decided that if we were making a buying mistake we were still young enough to work our way out of a disaster. I called the seller to accept his offering price. My voice must have vibrated too much eagerness. He immediately bumped the price ten percent higher. "Chump change," he said. He wasn't planning to leave "a nickel on the table."

"But," I said.

"Take it or leave it," he said.

We took it, and found ourselves wallowing in debt. Paying on time. Hoping for the best.

Years later the phone rings at my house, rousing me from a thoughtful moment while writing fiction on my laptop. I let it ring. I expect another solicitation—the usual requests for donations to good causes, perhaps a robo call, maybe the Democratic Party, or a local Republican Party candidate, or some problem with my credit card, possibly news that I'm a confirmed winner for a free trip to Hawaii.

The phone persists. The words in front of me lose their pull. My novel's protagonist slips away, pursued by the ringing phone, retreating to a lower order of my consciousness. Will I catch the last ring? I take the stairs two at a time down to the kitchen and yank the phone from its cradle.

"Mr. Trimakas?"

My worlds intersect. The boundaries of my fiction overlap and become confused. The character in my novel is new to Seattle, on the run and out of money. The man has booked an airport motel that rents rooms by the hour, and I stand in a white kitchen, surrounded by white tile, white counters, with a white phone in my hand, in a house overlooking Puget Sound.

The rhododendrons outside our house are heavy with blooms. The fluorescent white bundles hang in hallucinatory luminous skirts close to the ground.

"Mr. Trimakas?"

The man on the phone says he's a real-estate agent. He wants to know if the land on Highway 99 is still available.

"It's for sale."

Donna and I want to cash out. It's been on the market a while. But my voice must be soft. He doesn't hear me. I'm thinking of my story, of what happens next. I've just returned from Lee Smith's ("Oral History") fiction workshop at Duke University inspired to write a narrative outside my own life—Jolene, a pretty 7-Eleven clerk is exasperated with her partner on account of his habitual lying. Her partner reminds me of a salesman I'd once hired. He explains to Jolene that lying is a hugely creative act, vastly more challenging than telling the truth.

The real-estate agent nudges me toward another reality. "Will you consider a build to suit?"

The question arouses a mild defensiveness in me. The real-estate sign announces that I might indeed be willing, but that's only advertising, hinting at possibilities. Is he going to ask for a gambling casino? A topless dance club? Would Donna allow such a thing? Maybe only a go-cart track, or a miniature golf course?

"It's available," I say, raising my voice, breaking away from the novel, my commercial sense ascendant and the writer receding.

"A vehicle-type business," he says.

That could be anything. Used tires, junked motorcycles. A parts store. The telephone feels hot in my hand. "I prefer to sell." My voice suggests I'm not too eager to act even though I've been trying to develop, sell, trade, or lease the vacant land ever since we had bought it.

The real-estate agent says again that his client wants to locate a vehicle-type business on the site. Is he talking about car rentals? A junkyard for automobiles? He's not being specific, and that, too, is typical of cold-call inquiries. I haven't signed a real-estate listing agreement. I'm operating outside the agent's standard contract lockdown that guarantees an agent his commission. So we start with uncertainties, generalities, circling our mutual ignorance of each other.

The law in my state says that the real-estate agent works for you, the owner, unless he's working for both buyer and seller, or only for the buyer. But none of that is clear until the listing agreement is signed, and even then none of it is true either. What is always clear: The agent is working for himself or herself. We've established a conversational plateau—neither one of us trusts the other.

A part of me is still with the novel. A part of me watches our children's cat, Portia, undulate and rub against a corner of the refrigerator. The house remains empty, touched by the loneliness of a place recently vacated. Lisa, our daughter, has left for a summer job in the San Juan Islands. Our son Andrew has been gone since March on a three-month high school cultural exchange trip to France. Donna is at work at the printing store. I try for higher negotiating ground in a house abandoned by family. "I've had a lot of calls on that land," I say. I'm on to the game, a game of bluffs and calculations. "Are you sure your client is qualified?" Code words for: "Are we wasting our time? *Does he have the money?*"

"That's a good question," the agent says.

We've just built a tiny bridge toward openness. He doesn't identify his client. My conversation is on automatic now, lines from a script. I mention the benefits of the site, the local household income, population growth, and highway traffic count, the booming local employment in tech and aerospace companies. I could be a demonstrator pitching the benefits of a juicer sold at Costco.

Portia, bored with the refrigerator, rubs along the kitchen cabinets, bumping each panel with a languorous brush, looking for a handful of strokes from me. The cat used to ignore me, but with the children out of the house and Donna minding the printing business, I've become the hand of choice, an attendant to the small menagerie of pets—two dogs, a lovebird, a cat, koi in the pond—that she leaves behind each day.

"Will you finance?" The agent's intonations are casual.

"Maybe," I say.

I'm paying attention now. I'm also cash-poor. The printing company fields fifteen employees but is barely treading water. "Depends. Maybe short term. I won't subordinate though." That means I wouldn't take second position to any loans the buyer needs to borrow to build what he needs. Usually that's a deal breaker because banks are not likely to loan money to the buyer if they can't be in the first position to seize the property as security for nonpayment. But if I do agree and the buyers build and mortgage a building, and then bail on their loans, I have to pay off their loans or lose the property. I'm into risky behavior writing novels, but I'm not going to risk going broke. That's how it starts, a move, a countermove, a pause to think things over.

"I would like to show my client the site," the broker says.

I tell him to go ahead. He can do a drive-by, a walkabout. I don't have to be there. But I offer to show up if he needs me. I'm impatient to return to my writing, to get back to the world I'm imagining: the main character was abandoned when young. He's opportunistic, a liar, a dreamer, an occasional reactionary, and in love with his girlfriend. The novel is titled *Trust Me*.

The practical man within me says only a fool can be distracted by fiction. I'm not Bernard Malamud writing *The Natural*. I'm not a natural writer either, but I've fallen in love with my hard-pressed fictional characters.

The phone remains hot in my hand as the real-estate man waits for my answer. No one buys expensive slices of land on the lam or on a whim. I foresee meetings, soil tests, lawyers. Time spent with only a slim chance of success.

I take a deep breath. The story I'm writing may please no one. *Cut your losses,* the practical man says. The stubborn writer rejects advice. The issues become tangled. The hunt for money to support literary work gets shorted in our literature. I've not heard Jane Austin discuss it, though wealth and privilege are richly woven into her novels. Charles Dickens was much closer to the matter of money. In fact he was deep into it. His father went to debtor's prison. I imagine him shouting at me, "Talk to the real-estate guy on the phone!"

The page in front of me remains blank as I stand with a phone, talking. The broker says he'll get back to me if his client is interested. I return to the next thing Jolene wants to say to her lover.

10

THERE'S BEEN MORE CAREER AND BUSINESS ACTIVITY IN OUR lives than I've acknowledged so far. I've collapsed a number of years in my narrative. I've skipped most of the years Donna taught children at inner-city and suburban schools. I've elided my own corporate gig, to which I'll return. I've not mentioned several ventures that we'd hoped could go national, but never made it out of the neighborhood. The number of ventures we've explored trying to earn a living is daunting. We've taken a fling at operating a retail store, opened a second one, and then bailed out of both stores. Hip-hopping from one thing to another we had launched a garment screen-printing and manufacturing operation and another retail store, Rumpleshirtskin. (In the fairy tale, Rumplestilskin spins straw into gold.) The screen-printing operation employed several people and used automated equipment to print T-shirts, NFL shirts, and baseball shirts. We sold a good number of shirts, and then we sold that business too.

One year we plunged into consulting and seminars. We bailed out of a restaurant partnership just in time to keep us from going broke. For all of our effort we've been up and down on our business hobbyhorse too many times. The carousel went round and around and the brass ring was still out of reach. The newness of each venture, the uncertainty, the adventure of taking trips without maps or a precise destination was losing some of its charm.

Not unlike Joan Didion training to build shopping centers, we had hoped to build a self-sustaining moneymaking machine that would free our time to devote to other passions and goals. We were willing to prime the magical machine, oil it, stoke it along, and when the machine gathered steam we would have the money and the well-paid staff to run it, releasing us from day-to-day management to pursue our noncommercial ends.

We failed to become bohemians in the fifties (we were too young), or hippies in the sixties (we had to earn a living), punks in the seventies (our children needed us), or anarchists in the eighties (we were too busy). Nonetheless—we took a journey of many crossroads, divergent byways and narrow paths. Despite our up-and-down income, we've held on to each other and the vacant land north of Seattle—a city on the brink of explosive growth.

Meanwhile we're earthbound and busy. Commercial land gives off a feverish musky scent in an upmarket, raising the fever of speculators, the earnest attention of fee gatherers. The whispers go out, a national tenant is looking, and the Seattle metro region is hot. The news grows warmer in every conversation. "I can't tell who I'm representing," a broker might say. "We want confidentiality."

The sign I had erected on the land with my son's help says, "AVAILABLE." Smaller letters spell "Build To Suit." Though the plot is small, it is worth more than what Donna and I thought could ever be possible. It could be used as a down payment to secure a mortgage, converting land to something like cash. This compounding of wealth, untaxed, the wealthy call "appreciation." Though not wealthy we appreciate it, too. Our children remain oblivious to this booty. It's not something they can take to the 7-Eleven to buy a candy bar. As I look at the land that has never grown wheat or supported a garden I begin to see what lies underneath: new meanings, the hidden charm of financial freedom that it may suggest. Loan officers like to see the value posted on our financial statement, it lends belly, picturing a prosperous burgher, maybe someone Frans Hals might have painted.

But, we're cash-poor. The printing store Donna is managing full time hasn't paid her since we've launched—a measure of success that won't impress Wall Street. But for a self-financed neighborhood venture, our progress is promising.

A company with two or three employees has many local pleasures and is easy to manage, a business with more than fifty employees can be complex and needs experienced management. The companies falling between these two employment posts are often a purgatory of good intentions and many unmet challenges.

This is Main Street. Our neighborhood shop would seem to be an idyllic company, except the company doesn't earn much, but is large enough for employees to form cliques causing conflicts, some trivial, others unwieldy, all of them resolutely landing on Donna's desk.

We're into high complexity, fifteen computers networked in a small publishing environment. Our customers are interesting—the restaurant Hello Belly is a customer, a local National Public Radio station, along with local professionals, entrepreneurs and store managers. We take satisfaction knowing that Samuel Richardson, William Blake, Mark Twain and Benjamin Franklin once followed the printing trade.

We're at the store. The pristine white walls are hung with Mapplethorpe and Diego Rivera posters. "What's that smell?" Donna asks, alert, her chopsticks poised between bites of Chinese takeout. A folding machine that seizes stacks of paper and folds them into booklets is making a *shush clack clack* staccato sound. It's air-fed, uses steel platens, American made, and it usually works great. Her press operator tells her that the paper folder's motor is heating up. Donna tells him to order a new motor.

A shopkeeper's troubles intrude: John wants Friday off; Susan won't work Saturdays; Terry doesn't show up for work; Ahmad has a question about health insurance. Clay wants to know what he can do about his wages being garnished.

Okay, Donna will handle each question, each person, each problem, one after another. She has no sales manager, no service manager, no personnel manager, no printing manager, no computer manager, no accounting manager, no credit manager, no maintenance manager, no purchasing manager, no office manager, no marriage counselor either.

There's small business, and then there's really *small* business—we're in the latter group, and not for lack of trying to rise. Our effort reminds me of a gambling casino with no house percentage, no profit, an enterprise that suffers from too much service and not enough revenue.

Many, perhaps most, small-business owners are craftsmen for hire, laboring for a wage, but they believe otherwise, or hope otherwise. A small business when compared with a large "small" business is a very touchy vehicle to drive. We're not big enough to afford expert fees or large salaries. Donna and me, that's it. In the Orwellian redesign of language by lobbyists and lawyers working to benefit the super-wealthy and the fabulously rich we have redefined "small" business to favor huge family-owned multimillion dollar enterprises passed on through inheritance and legacy trusts meant to last centuries. Small has become big if you're a politician or lawyer hired to wash the feet of the rich.

But the vast majority of truly small business owners are the stepchildren of stepchildren when it comes to being helped by government policy decisions aimed to privilege the already rich.

Chrysler Motors stumbling on its many bad decisions can have Iacocca run to Congress for help to bail it out; General Motors and financial institutions badly mismanaged can also get help from Congress. But small businesses? Small-town dealerships? Operations like ours? The engines behind new job growth in America? You've got to be joking.

If you're managing such a business, you might want to think of yourself as riding a motorcycle, alert to each scent, the oil on the macadam, the slick grass in summer, the crack in the pavement. Anything can throw you over. A city planner coming along to propose a rezoning to outlaw your business. A bank imposing usurious conditions. Your most important employee leaving to work for a nearby competitor. You don't dare let go of the handlebars, the left hand always poised on the clutch, the right hand ready to brake. The ride is fun on a sunny day, a winding road, and on a long stretch, but too many days in Seattle are overcast.

We'd like to escape the trials of running a business, but how do you let go of the handlebars of a fast-moving motorcycle in the middle of the highway of your life?

We're collected for a staff meeting. Lots of good suggestions on how to spend more money, no suggestions on how to attract more business.

"You're undercapitalized," a staffer says.

I bite my tongue. What fool would risk as much? We've risked our savings, our time. We've risked lost opportunities and pleasures denied. We might be on the way to trading good health for bad. Who wants to hire so many people with no experience and train them for the next-larger company to come along and hire?

Here it comes: Donna, more free advice. You're overworked, killing yourself. Delegate, delegate, delegate, and *trust your staff, Donna!*

Okay, Donna gives it a try, she delegates more responsibility. Overtime blossoms like poppies in spring, deliveries lag. One of the staff extends more and more credit to his friends, nice people but like us, short of cash. Donna runs up her personal credit card to raise working capital to finance the accounts receivable. *Go for it, Donna!* She's leaning in, but actually, we're winging it.

The printing venture brings us into conflict. "This isn't how Onassis made his millions," I say.

She tells me to mind my own business.

I feel like a slacker, the unpublished novelist, bringing in no income. The Mondrian reproduction catches our attention—its dazzling optics, the jazz, the freedom. Can we ever get free of work?

"I got another call on the land," I say. "The real-estate man wouldn't tell me much." My words are a token of love, suggesting that help is near. The land remains our security, a chance for a jailbreak. It lies inert, an expensive slice of land on a commercial strip along a well-traveled road.

"How long would it take to sell the land?" she asks.

"I have no idea."

"I can't wait that long."

Dan Gustafson, her former principal in Highline School District, wrote in his evaluation: "Donna is one of those unusually effective teachers who is an unqualified asset to education. She enjoys children. She enjoys teaching. Her students enjoy learning. Her students enjoy Donna."

"Let's just sell the printing company," I say.

"Sell it?" she says. She goes to work early, works late. She loves the motion of people, the usefulness of enterprise. But money she doesn't understand. She likes to run the thing, the crises of enterprise, the hustle of customers coming and going and regrets the fact that we had sold her prospering pet store, Little Mermaid—pets that had fins and feathers and paws, a reflection of her inability to leave any living thing untouched by love, even the wooly tarantulas she kept in terrariums.

The Seattle Times reporter who interviewed her at the pet store got the story right: Small does not mean casual or easy. Little Mermaid's big draw was Charlie, a scarlet macaw. *The Science Times* reports that parrots "easily rival the great apes and dolphins in all-around braininess and resourcefulness, and may be the only animals apart from humans capable of dancing to the beat." Donna kept Charlie free to move on his perch and sometimes to walk about in the store. Unobserved by us, a clever Oscar Wilde, or perhaps a budding Phillip Larkin, taught Charlie to talk. Depending on Charlie's raucous mood, but often unprovoked, he could cast a beady eye on his fans and say, "Fuck you."

This didn't go over well with some customers, but the kids looking for tropical fish, hamsters, parakeets and canaries, giggled.

Business can be fun, more fun if you're earning money.

At home Donna sets out suet above the pond alongside our house for birds too lazy to fly south in the winter. The hummingbird feeder is hooked to a thermocouple to fire up a heating light to keep them warm just in case. This isn't tough love. She cares, attends to small and large things.

There seems to be no end to the work required to staff and run a small business. No scaling upward, no management teams, no investors looking to invest in mom-and-pop ventures, no venture capitalist looking at us as the next new thing, the Uber or Airbnb IPO valued at billions—we're actually dinosaurs, neither hip, nor cool, nor desirable. Yet small operations such as ours provide more than half of employment growth and possibly as many as two-thirds of all new jobs.

"I shouldn't have quit teaching," Donna says. "There are things that have gone out of me, pleasure and softness, but I don't know how to be hard."

"You're not alone, my love."

"No, I stand alone."

"Are we having an argument?"

She looks away.

"Let's hire a sales assistant admin-type to help."

We agree to start looking for someone, and I show up at the printing store more often. The geography of my mind divides into a confederation of fiercely opposed principalities. The first one is a region of numeric consequence, competition, niche markets, risk, margins, and costs. The thunder of percentages echoes in my mind, advertising and training, marketing and training, and more training—and in second place, writing, a region for the mind to wander uninhibited amid uncertain moments and fleeting emotions. The two principalities have no fence to clearly define them; one keeps expanding at the expense of the other.

There are similarities between writing a story and starting a new venture. Each requires courage to move beyond the reach of immediate sightlines, advancing from an uncertain beginning without seeing the distance you have to travel. With both, the work progresses in minute increments, details laboriously gathered, inspected, sorted for interest, and combined in some fashion to render a form. But commercial crises, no matter how suspect a month later, demand immediate attention. The novel sputters along.

11

THE REAL-ESTATE AGENT WANTS TO SEE ME AGAIN. HE COMES to our house. He reminds me of Paul Newman. We go to the kitchen. I pour him a cup of coffee.

"Nice view," he says, studying the waters.

Donna is at the printing store. I apologize for her giant fiddle-leaf fig soaring above the kitchen table, rising toward the ceiling. The agent takes the chair farther away to avoid the sensation of being trapped in a carnivorous plant.

"I have an offer," he says.

Did he say full price? Or did I just hear something that I wanted to hear? The agent's arched eyebrows rise a notch higher. He's too much of a gentleman to push for a stronger reaction. The hazards of commerce have brought us together. The royal blue logo on the front page catches my eye. "Is this the standard buy-sell form?" I'm searching for the security of a well-trodden path, accepted commercial norms to keep me safe, to preserve me from folly. The second page is not a preprinted page. Even to my inexperienced eye the tightly packed paragraphs look no more standard than a red-feathered seagull mooing. "How about the addendum?"

A bit reluctantly, he says, "The lawyer wanted that in." He touches his eyebrow, casually guiding me toward the next step. "Usually we get a counteroffer."

The offer is subject to his client's securing an unspecified franchise, not an unreasonable condition, except that it provides no date by which to achieve his success, which for all I know could take a year, or several years, but more significantly, the offer pays nothing for taking the land off the market while he attempts to arrange his fortunes.

Had I been more experienced in dealmaking I could have moved swiftly past the preliminaries, accepting, rejecting, suggesting, deleting paragraphs, or adding notes to the margins. But my working methods embrace ignorance; deliberation is my only preserve. I'll ride any straw on a rough sea, but I might not want to launch if I'm standing on the beach. My suspicion of commercial transactions is now reflexive, the shield of a misplaced person, the immigrant's protection. I say I need to think it over. I do nothing for a week. Then it becomes clear to me that the full-price offer is no offer at all. It's a buyer's option that may or may not be exercised.

I wait. Again I do nothing.

The real-estate agent calls once more. No longer as cautious or reserved about his client as he had been at first, he says flat out that his client wants to build a new car dealership. The country is flooded with over six hundred models of cars. Sixty-seven percent of dealerships have gone out of business since the glory car days after World War II, and the immediate economic future looks a bit dodgy. I'm curious to see a man so inclined to move against the grain. I learn his name is Bollinger. We agree to meet him at the site.

Being first or last at such meetings can lead to foolish just-in-time complications. Questions of who has the edge and who is more eager to buy or sell are weighed by the passage of minutes. It's all somewhat childish when timeliness and professionalism command attention and the fashionably late are no longer in fashion.

I arrive early. It's a cool, sunny day as I walk in the tall grass before the meeting. Vivid yellow Scotch broom is scattered about to add joy to the day. A large Douglas fir grows on the south decline. I check in with a neighboring landowner who runs a furniture store. He tells me a homeless person has fashioned a plywood shelter under the fir, a home surrounded by scrub. "I've asked him to clean up for me." He checks his watch doubtfully. "The guy may not show up." We both look at the thick growth. "He says he's an engineer, something mechanical. Talks intelligent." He draws a breath and lets out a half sigh. "Supposedly he has family back East."

It makes us pause. No wild-assed artist this homeless man. No wannabe writer without a job. My colleague and I shudder at the thought of a middle-class college-educated man becoming homeless. "The police checked him out," my neighbor says. "They can't do anything as long as the owner doesn't complain."

I'm the owner. I haven't complained. We squint at the sun and ponder the circumstances without coming to grips with it.

My neighbor leaves. The real-estate agent and Bollinger pull up in separate vehicles. Bollinger owns a Cadillac dealership but is driving humbly today, just one of the guys, in a pickup truck. He would tell me later that he knew he was in trouble when a reporter assigned by *The Seattle Times* to do a profile on him drove up in a car that had a bumper sticker that read: "SAVE THE WHALES, EAT THE RICH."

He leaps out of the pickup and moves quickly, appraising me briskly, perhaps thinking of matters back at his dealership. He's a robust-looking man—broad face, light skin, ruddy cheeks, blonde hair, and an eager glad-to-know-you manner. His handshake starts with an exposed palm (indicating he's unarmed, open to friendship, ready to deal). His voice is vigorous. He looks happy to see me. He doesn't know how very happy I am to see him. We check the site. I guide my visitors away from the homeless man's residence. The man can stay into the winter, or until he can pay for an apartment, or until the bulldozers come to prepare the land for luxury cars.

Dealerships prefer open acreage angled toward the highway to display inventory to drivers speeding on a busy state road. I'm not the best site available, but in the parlance of auto guys, Bollinger is not a tire kicker. He gives the site's awkward features a cursory inspection, and a few minutes later we're heading for the Taco Bell a hundred feet distant. There's a small skirmish at the cash register. Big spenders, the three of us want to pop for the price of the taco meal. But we each pay for our own four-dollar meal to establish our independence.

Deals between strangers are precarious shifting events that can slip away at the slightest unexpected ill breeze. Commerce has a form— there's a fashion on Wall Street, another in Hollywood, and variations of my Main Street meeting with Bollinger in the rest of the country—but the structure is often unpredictable. I don't usually ask personal questions. Not usually. I try to meet expectations. I've left my Mickey Mouse watch at home. My sports jacket is appropriately somber, and I suppress my journalistic curiosity.

With a salesman's graceful skill Bollinger glides closer to common ground. "Would you build a building for me?" he asks in a quick aside, as if this were the last thing on his mind. His real-estate agent hadn't offered any details.

"I'm looking to cash out," I say.

The three of us are remarkable for being so unremarkable. Ordinary is highlighted. No Italian suits, no English tailoring. No monograms on our shirtsleeves. Nothing fashionable. We don't have New York City's famous La Grenouille restaurant in Seattle (although we have fine restaurants) and no one of national stature to see or be seen with, unless you mean Bill Gates, who in his earlier days didn't have a private security company fielding a phalanx of guards to keep him safe as he stood solo next to a Tower Books magazine rack.

The real-estate agent says they'd negotiated for three months on another location before giving up. On the face of that comment I'm second on their list, but more likely I'm third or fourth. I'm the wallflower asked out for a spin. It makes me lightheaded.

The site they like has a small building on it. I explain that I would need to subdivide the site and sell them only the vacant portion, but they tell me that won't give them the two acres the car manufacturer demands before granting a franchise. The real-estate agent seems to lose his appetite. Bollinger can't finish his taco. I'm not sure if the cola in my hand is too cold or the blood has left my hands. We offer smiles all around and promise to keep in touch. But I hear the sounds of a final goodbye. I must be their Plan B, the backup plan. They're hunting for something better.

At home, I say to Donna, "This could have paid for our sabbatical, maybe a long stay at a writers' colony."

"Have a drink," she says.

We can be ferociously intimate, or exhausted, depending on which way the winds at work had been blowing that day. We toast good cheer to each other, start kissing, and take to the bedroom to make love. In the morning she says, "Wasn't that more fun than a stay at a writers' colony?"

12

NEED TO CHECK THE CITY'S SUBDIVISION REQUIREMENTS IN CASE another buyer comes along. You walk up to the Planning Department as you would walk up to the sales counter of a department store, and you wait if there's a line. Today there's no line. "You've got parking requirements, building-to-lot coverage ratios, fire truck access problems," the city planner says. He's saying it's nearly impossible to subdivide the land and leave enough parking for Bollinger. "You can ask the city council for a variance," he says. The professional distance in the man's eyes tells me I'd be wasting my time.

I meet Donna at the printing store. She shrugs away the failed effort. A chapter thrown out. The land remains mute, commercial, immovable. "Bollinger might come around if we agree to sell him the existing building *and* the vacant land."

"What's our other option?"

We both know the answer. More laboring, more tension.

But weeks float by with minimum stress. Time passes. It's the beginning of a beautiful summer. Her firecracker energy sparkles at home and at work. She's on the front lines of our printing venture. There's no R&R in a business our size, no limited tour. When you sign up it might be for life.

I'm on the line to Bollinger once again. "I've been thinking," I say. "Since I can't divide the land into a smaller portion that'll make your car manufacturer happy, maybe you can buy the vacant land *and* the small building on it? That'll give you slightly more than two acres." I name a price.

But, no, it turns out he can't buy the land.

I push the mute button on the phone and ask Donna, "How do you feel about going on the hook for his mortgage and build him what he needs?"

"Be his landlord?"

"It's a job."

"The banker told us not to do it."

"What else can we do?"

She humors me. "I can sing, you can dance. We'll escape."

"And take the kids?"

"I'm not sure they need us anymore."

"We'll take the dogs?"

"We couldn't do otherwise."

"And Cho-Cho, too."

"You want to take the lovebird?"

"Everyone comes."

I get back on the phone with Bollinger. "Maybe I can develop the thing for you?"

He says we should talk.

We meet the next day, and in a rush of familiarity shake hands with the enthusiasm of two happy otters. He suppresses the boyish good humor that often seems close to his surface. We've both run through a number of years in our lives. His surprise seems to linger longer than mine.

By my estimate, we have only a one-in-ten chance of doing business together. We don't know how expensive his building will be. Neither one of us knows for sure if we can raise the money each of us needs: his working capital, my mortgage to build his building. He has never successfully run more than one rooftop (slang for a single building that may house two auto brands). But we're a little chattier than we were earlier.

He's charming and stoutly handsome, a third-generation auto dealer from Walla Walla, a small town, a city surrounded by aquifers and agriculture, vineyards, croplands, forests, grasslands near the border of Oregon and Washington. It's a sunny place, and in summer the temperatures can hit one hundred degrees Fahrenheit. The grassy park-like South Palouse Street is shaded by American elm, American sycamore, and silver maple. The maples can grow higher than sixty feet. It's a town that loved itself so much that in a stutter of affection it named itself twice, *The home of the Walla Walla sweet onion.*

Bollinger grew up amid the town's many charms, trading on his dad's local auto dealership success. He's a man of the West. As Arthur Chapman says in his poem, "Out where the handclasp's a little stronger, / Out where the smile dwells a little longer, / That's where the West begins." Bollinger is also a Wazoo (WSU-Washington State University) grad and a big-time Cougar football fan. That's a contact sport. A game of domination, violence and conquest. Brains get damaged. His dad and his mom had graduated from Wazoo too. All his children would go to Wazoo and become Cougar fans. The Cougars would one day adopt his third wife as an honorary Cougar. The family outlier in this home team is his sister, who went to Stanford.

Donna's and my sports credentials are thin by comparison. Our families fielded a librarian, a poet, a musician, a transcontinental bridge builder, a judge, artists, teachers, patriots of several passions, a political leader, and several men of the cloth. No one claimed to be a writer, or a sportsman. Donna, though, had mastered the killer shot in a game of marbles, and the hop-skip technique to land inside hopscotch boxes chalked on the sidewalk. I confess to playing stickball, and collecting Yankee and Dodger baseball cards when I was young.

Our son, who'll be on the University of Washington Husky football team when they get to play the Rose Bowl, says we suffer from a sports attention deficit disorder (SADD). What's more, I have a curious obsession: I like to write, I want to write, become a writer. A dodgy way to earn a living. I mention my interest in writing a nonfiction book about risky Main Street commerce to Bollinger. He humors me and promises to send me his personal financial statement "if you don't laugh at it." I smile, which is what he expects me to do. We shake hands. Bollinger says that we have an "agreement to agree."

13

THE ENERGY DEVOTED TO MAIN STREET PROJECTS GIVES ME an idea for a nonfiction book. I loved Tracy Kidder's book, *House*, in which the owners and an architect and a builder work toward a common goal. I write a sketch and show it to Bollinger. He likes it. I'm encouraged to write a book proposal, pitching the idea to literary agents. Afterward, I attend a writers' workshop in Colorado, led by the celebrated writer Geoffrey Wolff, widely known for his memoir about his father, *The Duke of Deception*.

I'm a fan of the self-help industry, classes and books, workshops and seminars—organized to tell you how to do this and how to avoid that. The participants are often engaging, and we get to choose the workshop we want to attend, in my case mostly fiction workshops.

As Morris Dickstein explains in his preface to *Leopards in the Temple* he became "as enamored of novels as kids later did of rock music, movies, or favorite TV shows." He wanted, as a young man, "to rub shoulders with other people in other worlds, to find out what would happen next." I was hooked, too. Stories are travel guides to lands and people we might not otherwise ever visit. Eudora Welty in *One Writer's Beginnings*, says that "Writing fiction has developed in me an abiding respect for the unknown in a human lifetime and a sense of where to look for threads, how to follow, how to connect ..."

But how to begin a literary journey in midlife?

This is what led me to Geoffrey Wolff at Aspen, to Tim O'Brien at Sewanee, the wonderful Lee Smith at Duke University, the celebrated and cerebral Margaret Atwood at Centrum, the iconic Frank Conroy in Iowa, Richard Ford in Park City, Utah, and to Eileen Myles's evening poetry workshop in Manhattan. I've taken a tour of the United States to catch up with identity and gender politics, and literature.

In Wolff's workshop we're talking about ethics, about truthfulness, deception, and fair play in the nonfiction arena. The oxygen is roughly twenty or thirty percent less than you would find at sea level in Seattle. I'm troubled by a slight headache, a condition I'm told will surrender itself to the good mountain air in a few days.

Wolff leans back from the table and takes a breath, inhaling with a shudder. "I'll never do it again," he says, talking about his book-proposal experience. "Oh," he says, swaying, rolling his head. He did it once. Sold one of his books on a skillfully written book proposal. He'd taken the advance money and suffered the writing, suffered the editor, and he promised not to do it again.

I see a fine writer, admired, long-established, distinguished, relaxed in the traditions of academia and literary friendships. He has writers and editors participating in his workshop, along with a wayward soul or two. I'm one of the wayward souls. My literary background is thin. Every new book I read, even if published a century earlier, strikes me as wonderful. I'm tiptoeing my way into a field of uncertainties, spotting daffodils where someone else might see thorns. I'm aiming for skill. But by the time I start attending writing workshops, I'm so late starting a writing career that the joke might be I'm a half-century late. I might even win a medal for late starters.

Once more I'm a beginner.

The "creative" teaching trade has produced an industry supplied with associations, conventions, leaders and followers, acolytes and gurus, movements and literary schools enough to baffle any novice—a market that offers residencies, teaching assistantships, grants, tenured positions and on occasion, directorships. But if the creative gene is missing from a hopeful writer, and you're seeking to write imaginative work, no amount of advice or word-association exercises is going to make you creative. These confusing contradictions have driven many to contemplate suicide. And some have followed through.

If you happen to go to a writers' conference unanchored to your sense of self, unsure of your ability, untutored, and without mentors— the typical conditions surrounding novice writers—each workshop you visit, every opinion you hear, each literary breeze and jittery comment will blow you along as if you were a dandelion, scattering the seeds of what might have been distinctive over a field too wide for anyone to see what was once original.

Flannery O'Connor is instructive. Startlingly original, she declined to work with an editor mired in conventional attitudes, and thus we have *A Good Man Is Hard to Find*. She's a good counselor to follow.

Part of the protocol at writers' conferences is to remain silent as other writers plunge to be helpful with sabers and chisels, sheers and scalpels to excise your sins by critiquing a sample of your writing. The underlying purpose is to improve your work. The process, though, is generally one of opinionated destruction. The piece by piece picking apart of workshop samples is meant to help everyone attending, everyone fishing for morsels to chop.

But the approach is deeply flawed as an educational tool applied to labors configured as creative. In any conflict between creation and destruction, the latter is quicker. If you're a critic, destruction is not only easier, it can be more fun, and the stiletto-sharp critical one-liner more memorable.

Maureen Corrigan, author of *So We Read On*, and an insightful National Public Radio literary critic, says young critics typically outgrow their elbow-first tendencies as they mature. The internet, though, is a space for Twitter-style criticism where no one needs to ever grow up should they choose not to do so. The internet has democratized every-man as a critic, an admirable event, and also enabled an army of hashtags billowing ten-second takedowns.

For the writer, what to build, and how to build it is the challenge. There's no diploma, no conclusive act to reward good work. Building fiction and narrative prose requires design, attention to detail, struc-ture, pacing, conflict, background, a sense of place, an interior view of the people involved, and the exterior forces pushing them. To weigh and assess and compare what goes into such work and then render an informed opinion requires much work. The critics who prepare themselves for this demanding, poorly paid, daunting task are a gift to culture.

The critic Wayne C. Booth offered the most valuable piece of advice I've not heard voiced in a workshop: "What they [writers] have yet to learn, if they know only this, is the art of choosing what to dramatize fully and what to curtail, what to summarize and what to heighten. And like any art, this one cannot be learned from abstract rules."

Yet workshops are full of spoken and unspoken rules, some that I support. Onto these shifting tectonic plates I've placed my hopes. In the workshop group I'm the outsider wanting in. The barriers are up, suspicions examined. I've been here before. The grade-school clumsy speller, the high-school poet good enough to antagonize my teacher into asking me who wrote the poem for me. Becoming, becoming, always becoming. The group reads the introduction to my book proposal:

> At forty-five Bollinger is a third-generation auto dealer. He's a large man with fair skin and his pink cheeks are glowing. I like his energy, his robust laugh, and his eagerness to play for high stakes. We've been arguing for ten minutes, each of us stepping on the other's words, tripping on a train of emotion. We cannot agree on how much risk should be mine and how much should be his. He grabs the arm of his chair, lets go and rocks forward, locking his large hands to keep them under control. We're on the rim of a multi-year, multimillion-dollar deal, an amount freighted with fabled meaning, half-mirage, half-possibility.

I wait for a response, uneasy, partly proud of this modest effort, partly embarrassed, unable to position my work near the fine writers I've read and admired. I've earned my keep far from public largesse and private-trust income, unspoiled by charitable tenures, far from the privileges of academia and study overseas. I'm close to the friction of money changing hands. This is not the profile of most participants in my group.

A participant returns my offering with a scribbled note in the margin: *I stopped reading here!!!* Sitting in front of me he fingers his pen. I get it. He doesn't like what he's read. He doesn't say why, or how to fix it. Probably, he doesn't know, but he doesn't like it nonetheless. I don't know why he doesn't like it. But to make his point, during the oral portion of the criticism, he says, "It didn't work for me."

The samples offered at workshops are often taken as self-revelation. This tends to push participants, me included, toward anxiety. My critic works in landscaping. Maybe he bicycles, and dislikes car lots. Resentment can grow in such circumstances, and money-consciousness runs deep.

The protocol requires me to say, "Thank you." I'm thinking, *Thank you my ass*, but I don't say it. I go on about other things, my voice probably confident and quick, a manner I've long-managed, especially when I'm least sure of my prospects. The group waits a moment; unease keeps us attentive, provisional. Then we move on to another writer's offering.

The critic and literary historian Harold Bloom, among many other critics, weighed in on the merits of creative writing programs. He says they probably do more good than harm (as in my case), but it distresses him to think what could have been lost to literature had Herman Melville brought *Moby Dick* to a writing workshop.

At home, once more out on our deck overlooking Puget Sound, Donna throws some light on the criticism. "He didn't care what you wrote. He was pissed off at *you* for mentioning the million dollars involved. You should have told him it's an exploration of cultural values. Our marriage."

"That would have blown his fuckin' mind."

But she's right. The writing introduced at workshops is often incidental. The writer is the true subject.

Before the term "microaggression" had been coined, most of us experienced put-downs, slights. It's the verbal traffic we deal with if we want to live in a diverse and vibrant nation. Setting aside my own work, there are larger issues at stake. To pretend that cruel prejudices and heinous acts do not exist by allowing students safe spaces where they will never hear about them, nor respond to the carriers of such cultural diseases, is to prepare students to live in a utopian world that doesn't exist.

I had a writing teacher who introduced my offering to the class with a rhetorical query: "What are we to do with this beautiful dishrag?" (She got an A from me for wit.) Another teacher took the trouble to slip me a class-conscious kill pill by categorizing my work as "petit bourgeois." The *petit* had bothered me more than the *bourgeois*, which I took to mean "middle-class."

By the time I started writing *Car Palace* I had learned to separate the work from the author, but putting that knowledge into practice is difficult. I keep trying nonetheless. Dodging bullets—slings and arrows, if you wish—is part of the engagement when you post your work in the public square.

A writer's beginnings are always tenuous. I'm a novice writer after passing through a wide array of novitiates: the immigrant kid, the Army soldier, a foreman, the Boeing computer systems analyst, an executive, a husband, a father, a self-employed retailer, and eventually the nontraditional "returning" student. Each novitiate has its own floors to mop, windows to wipe, expenses to pay, and bosses to avoid.

I can generalize that most border jumpers attempting cultural crossings such as Donna and I had attempted are not often welcomed on either side of the border. We're traitors to one side, unwelcome on the other side. At many border crossings the native guards complained, resisted, raised barriers. To some we were intruders, outliers, the uninvited. This book is partly about such radical instability, and our attempts to smooth the path as we moved beyond our own immigrant community.

Our journey was sometimes derailed by competing energies on the way to becoming this, that, or another thing in our lives. Some of these transitions were internal, fighting the enemy within. We weren't educated in the democratic pluralism we now admire and inhabit. We were trained in moral absolutes—we would go to hell for eating meat on Fridays, for missing church on Sundays. Hell was for eternity. You couldn't just visit hell, point out that you've made a mistake, and then leave. In one cultural jailbreak after another, we trained ourselves to break with foolish beliefs.

Cultural travel also animates our creative spirit. In my case it feeds a boisterous skepticism, bolsters a satiric stance, and shapes my literary materials, which doesn't impress Donna. She asks, "Could you take up tennis instead of writing?"

She knows the story I'm about to tell.

My friend Billy Squier had introduced me to his friend the tennis star John McEnroe when we met McEnroe at a restaurant on the Upper West Side of Manhattan. Given my laggard sports curiosity I hadn't heard of McEnroe, which led to an awkward moment after I asked McEnroe what he did for a living. He was unsettled, as if the shaft of light he had been riding had suddenly dimmed. Maybe he was torn between thinking me a fool and being polite to his, and my, friend Billy.

Donna smiles. "Can you take up golf?"

I don't golf either.

Border crossings are never easy, jailbreaks even more trying.

According to the critic Susan Sontag men can be divided into lovers or husbands. My position with Donna seems to be shifting. "I get it. I get it," I say. "I'm wasting my time at workshops." The ship-lighted waters on the Sound in front of us shimmer with beauty. We hug.

14

THE BOLLINGER DEAL BUMPS ALONG. DONNA REMINDS ME
that very early in my immigrant life I've attended a Dale
Carnegie course. Carnegie's best-selling book *How to Win
Friends and Influence People* is famously described by a critic writing
for *The Nation* as "the best outline of the science of tail-wagging and
hand-licking ever written."

It's not surprising that Bollinger had taken a Dale Carnegie course,
too. The both of us indulged our inner Dale Carnegie at different times
and for different reasons. Bollinger, self-described as a "people-person"
and already a winner in the likability sweepstakes, took the class to
be more likable. He was moved to reinforce his strengths. I took it to
learn American salesmanship, a move to overcome a weakness.

He sends me reports from *Automotive News*, and several brochures
printed by the car manufacturer. I'm more conscious of the tiny crack
in my car's windshield and the new cars on the road. So many new
cars. Glossy, sleek, iridescent with the good life. When I see him at his

Cadillac dealership, I park on the street. I don't want him to compare my well-oiled wreck with the new models he sells.

He has engaged my interest, telling me freely of his own uncertainty, mentioning his bad experience with a failing Tri-Cities dealership he once owned. He survived the debacle by off-loading the unprofitable dealership on someone else. To make the sale palatable, he called himself inexperienced, suggesting that someone as competent as the buyer could become profitable.

Say what you will about this mea culpa maneuver, and think what you wish, but it's not unusual to want someone to share the burden of our mistakes after we've made them.

Bollinger and I are happy words well into the summer, but we don't have anything in writing. It's all speculation. I've not heard him swear or raise his voice in anger over our lack of progress. As we sit closer to the levers of soft money pumping wealth, I edit my speech to remove the four letter words learned in Brooklyn and the US Army. His Cadillac dealership financial statements show bracketed numbers around the category "cash." The brackets indicating a cash hole are off-putting if you're a banker, but to the business operator it's an expression of confidence in the future, writing checks and holding them until cash receipts catch up to fill the cash hole. A practice we follow at the printing store, thus the brackets suggesting a bucket of optimism waiting to be filled.

We should have some firm numbers by now, but we don't. Either I'm dragging my feet, or he is. Back and forth we go. Our *mano-a-mano* meetings leave me satisfied and vaguely uneasy. Who's on first base, who's on second? Who knows? I've broken my own rules, other people's rules, rejected sound commercial advice: take the money, insist on it, sell the land and run. But without other options to tempt Donna and me, the car palace project looks more promising each passing week, and profit is always a siren.

Bollinger offers an opinion on how much the building should cost. I pitch a possible rent figure based on the cost. He draws a finger across his lips in contemplation. He smiles, but I'm not sure if he's agreed, or is just being friendly. I mention that the venture is risky, but I've also become an advocate, justifying a higher rate of return. To distance myself from my own wallet, I say his real-estate agent provided the market info. Nothing is decided. Neither one of us has gained or lost anything except some sleep as we keep playing Monopoly.

15

GEOFFREY WOLFF WEARS A WESTERN BUCKLE, PERHAPS because we're in Colorado. "Oh, no, no," he says, relaying again the slight anguish he suggests with his pauses. He is troubled that some of us want to sell a book to a publisher by crafting our pitch in a book proposal, which I'm attempting.

Unlike many less experienced writers and workshop leaders he doesn't overwhelm you with advice. He chooses what to say very carefully. He says that I'm withholding too much in my memoir. Memoirs often offer some unexpected moment intimately lived. I admit that a full-on confessional mode is not my automatic mode, or first choice. As a child of an alcoholic parent I've developed an unprotected child's tight boundaries, keeping my secrets secret. Chief among them was a fear that my mother would show up drunk. No matter that I loved her, I was afraid to brings friends to the house. A family hazard that I could not reveal were she still alive. Which only proves that many writers are braver than me, including the remarkable and talented Kathryn Harrison, who gave us the memoir *The Kiss*, describing a consensual affair with her father.

But there's another side to the transparency debate. If transparency in government is essential for us to judge the policies of fools eager to lead us into wars, a citizen's privacy rights is the other side of the coin. Without privacy, and the expectation of privacy, shared intimacy would be impossible. All of us would be wondering who will say what in public the next morning. I'm reminded of Edgar Allen Poe, *The Imp of the Perverse*: "I am safe—I am safe—yes—if I be not fool enough to make open confession!"

I've persuaded a literary agent to send my *Car Palace* proposal to several editors. The queries get a response. An editor praises the writing but doesn't know where the book is headed—a good observation, neither do I. Not knowing exactly what lies ahead is how I've started venturing, hoping to learn enough along the way to avoid disaster. A pattern that at times may be linear, but most often is not. You search and test, skip a step, jump a line, repeat, add a variation and hope for the best. This approach requires healthy bones and a stable mind to endure many pratfalls. Ambiguity is common at the beginning of each venture, uncertainty another friend. The two precede me in each project as I check the ground for gopher holes, rattlesnakes and scorpions, lions, tigers, and bears.

The literary agent, meeting resistance from an editor, breaks protocol by giving the editor my phone number to see if we're a match. The editor calls and muses, "My colleagues will wonder ..."

I misunderstand completely what's about to happen. I'm neither famous nor accomplished as a writer. The editor is interviewing me to see if I'm worth his time and trouble. "I like your work," he says to smooth the tense conversation. I hear him praise *Car Palace* as a lively three-ring circus. He speaks firmly, assured of directions, of colleagues, of publishing. I lose his clear speech in the weeds of my anxiety. I know nothing. The workshops don't cover this territory. The underlying premise of writing workshops seems to be: You'll never get published, but we'll have a lot of fun on the path to this discovery.

In my business conversations I have vendors, customers, clients, friends, guys. We're mostly indie operators. Not once has anyone addressed me as "colleague," a word reserved for a privileged group of insiders, professionals employing a specialized language, and shared goals. I listen to the editor and picture flowing robes, crimson and magenta, white and yellow, mortarboards, and capes, yes, beautiful capes that my father wore among colleagues, a solid wall of skeptics.

Professionals in the publishing industry say that traditional publishers, what we now call "legacy" publishers, an oligarchy of five global media corporations, publish fewer than two percent of manuscripts submitted. The editor would like to know how to run a dealership. I haven't a clue how to run a dealership, and I'm not interested in running a dealership. That's Bollinger's job. My job is to judge his character and evaluate his competence to succeed with his plans.

The editor still wants a how-to book.

Dealerships depend on two talents the owner and operator must posses, the talents of the salesman, and those of the businessperson. The salesman is the helpful person that you trust for their information and service, the man or woman who sells you the car, offers financing, and accepts your trade-in; the businessperson must spin and juggle the many wheels of customer demand and employee needs, mindful of the manufacturers' marching orders, bank and landlord requirements. The sales task is not so simple but straightforward, the business part is complex. But even with both talents abundantly present the dealer has limited power over his or her own success. What brings a dealership remarkable success is a car the public is eager to buy. Building such a desirable car—applying the creative work of designers and engineers and marketing gurus to satisfy evolving consumer needs—resides exclusively with the manufacturer.

The editor has a vision of what the book should be. I have another. There's a peculiar doubling of energies as we talk, even a double-mind-edness. If visions could be made astral I could name our conversation *Visions Collide!* But I say "yes" to his query almost involuntarily, automatically, the salesman within me not wanting to lose a sale. And then I describe the opposite of what he wants. The editor talks quickly. I sense he has other calls to make. I suspect he's made up his mind. Or perhaps it's only the New York tempo and it's nearly four o'clock in Manhattan.

"I don't think running a dealership is all that interesting," I finally say. "The creative part of the industry relies on good manufacturing and marketing decisions." Unhappy with my flatfooted denial of another's opinion I go on, "The unknown risks, conflicting expectations, attitudes, the printing startup, our marriage and tensions, family, all these threads, the conflicts ..." I stumble on, resolutely incoherent. The wrong words are stitched to my tongue, repetitive, hesitant, macaroni and cheese instead of pasta and prosciutto, idiom collapses, tenses running loose. I'm reduced to the list of ten words, four of them misspelled that Sister Thomas is pointing out to my father as the reason to keep me back a grade. Learning a language is always a challenge, learning a culture more so. The two play tag with each other, affecting each other, adjusting conventions, enforcing obedience, sometimes opening doors, sometimes encouraging prejudice. The nun kept me back a grade on account of my misspellings. The intervention failed to help my spelling.

"I've got what I need to know," the editor says firmly.

The voice I hear isn't inviting me to join the club. For all I know, his father owns a string of dealerships. Maybe he was John Updike's editor when Updike created his auto-dealer Rabbit books? Maybe he heard that the choreographer Twyla Tharp's father was a Ford dealer? Wait, wait,

I want to say. There's more. Kurt Vonnegut owned a Saab dealership on Long Island. He taught a class at NYU that Donna attended. Yes, yes, I want to say, if John McPhee can write a book about oranges, surely I can say more about dealerships.

The editor lets me down gently, "I'd like to see your fiction. Maybe your agent will show it to me?"

I hear a crock of friendly frogs looking to escape. He doesn't want to offend the agent who'd sent him my proposal. I call the agent and tell her the conversation wasn't promising. It doesn't trouble her. She has other clients, paying clients.

"I could be wrong," I say, looking for a seed of hope. "David Mamet, you now, like *Glengarry Glen Ross*, big-ticket sales, a group of salesmen?" I'm thinking about the messiness of deals, the greed, the cowardice, everyone excited, throwing dice, yet hoping to control the uncertain impulses of commerce, some of which brings us a measure of beauty, along with great stores of useful product, along with lots of litter, all of this mingled, hopelessly mixed …

I realize my agent is not listening.

"Maybe dealerships *are* interesting?" I volunteer.

She stops me from beating myself up. "Another editor wondered if you could pick another subject altogether, at least not anything about dealerships." She's showing me the size of the new arena, much larger than any writer's workshop. In the background of my mind I hear Geoffrey Wolff's soft, suffering, "Oh."

16

'VE LOST MY BEST CHANCE TO SELL A BOOK. WHAT NOW? Deciding what to do next finds us looking for a workaround. This is a familiar pattern for many of us. There are plenty of roadblocks in life. Few goals are seized from ill fate on the first effort.

When our daughter Lisa turns twelve, she shows a startling drop in school interest. She's not attending a school for the underprivileged. There is a full-size track at school, a soccer field, a gymnasium, tennis courts, music teachers, and we have underpaid student advisers, too. Lisa's adviser says to us confidentially, "If I had the money. I'd send my kids to a private school." Regardless of my misspellings, for which I don't blame the schools, I'm a product of a mostly public education. Her suggestion unsettles us.

We live on the outskirts of Seattle in a community where professional men and women jog in electric green running outfits and iridescent blue running shoes before stopping at Starbucks. Many houses have garages to hold four cars, and people are more concerned about the trees that block their views than they are about national defense.

The neighborhood grapevine informs us that we should ask the school to reassign Lisa to another teacher. We hustle off to talk to the principal. I wear my conservative PTA suit. My otherwise longish hair is trimmed. I'm as establishment as good camouflage can ever make me feel. We're pleading our case on behalf of Lisa. Astonishingly, the principal argues that at *his* school, all the teachers are excellent, or extremely good.

"Okay," I say.

He hears my silent doubts. Then we exchange a few words. I know he can't mean what he's just said, not totally. He's a proponent of the non-judgmental approach to education, a groupthink approach, intellectual socialism growing unchecked in suburban America. I half expect him to say that at *his* school, all students are equal in talent, in scholarship, in ambition and dedication. He pretends not to know what I'm getting at. But whatever that might be he doesn't like the sound of it.

I wait for him to explain. Donna waits.

He snaps his head to the side, as if to avoid a blow. Dislike subverts his face, disorganizes the pleasant look he wears as casually as a cardigan sweater. "Hit the road, if you don't like it here."

I blink. Quite literally, I blink. I also sit up. Hit the road? I can almost hear him say, *Another fucking immigrant.*

Though Donna's and my immigrant identity is a distant curiosity to our children, events keep intruding to remind us otherwise. A month after the horrors of 9/11, we found ourselves in Manhattan watching a parade organized to boost the morale of Manhattanites living south of Fourteenth Street. The pulverized air was still acrid. Emotions were high and intense. The parade stumped its way along Broadway. A beautiful young woman was riding on top of a Humvee, waving an American flag, and shouting "Fucking immigrants" at no one in particular.

We're Americans. If we're not insiders, no one takes us for outsiders either. We pass. But at the edges of our perception, on oblique angles, on a "slant" as Emily Dickinson might say, we're still immigrants, always wary.

The principal brings us back to Lisa's trouble in school. "We're not an education boutique," he says.

Okay. I get it. I've been pushing him too hard. My suburban camouflage must have failed me—the bourgeois suit, the neat haircut. Brooklyn Tech, City College of New York, Regents' Scholarship, the GI Bill of Rights paid for a master's degree, but always a Bed-Stuy kid. Let's try Donna: the selective Girls High graduated her, then Temple University, not exactly log cabin material. We carry politically correct baggage, except now we should hit the road. Perhaps I shouldn't have spoken to the principal as if we were shopping at a bazaar known for shoddy goods that held a monopoly on good intentions.

Donna looks distracted, concentrating on keeping the wetness in her eyes from spilling over. "I'm just, I'm ... we're trying ..." She can't get it out. The tears come closer. "We want Lisa to have a good education."

The principal nods his head, relieved by Donna's interruption. Our man-to-man thing wasn't working for us. He's happy to make a switch. It allows us to gather our social wits, withdraw our horns, soften our words, and assert a common interest: education of children. Who can be against that? The principal regrets his hit-the-road comment. Perhaps he's had a difficult day. Within minutes, he's in full retreat and promises to reassign Lisa to another teacher.

Outside, the track isn't being used, the playing field absorbs a thin wash of sunshine and Lisa's adviser's suggestion lingers with us: "If I had the money, I'd send my kids to a private school."

17

MY COMMERCIAL EDUCATION STARTED EARLY. AFTER MY TASTE of door-to-door salesmanship selling Collier's books and Gerber baby food, the interlude spent working for a consumer finance company and then Big Steel, I looked for a change in employment. One company's advertising promoting "Great Ideas of Western Man" caught my attention. The ads are as artful today as they were then—I kept a complete set in a commemorative package—promoting Emerson, Thoreau, Montaigne, Einstein, Santayana, and many more—almost the entire Western canon, each with an original work of art commissioned by the company.

Time magazine ran one of those ads showing a painting by Clark Richert who was twenty-two at the time. This work, an evocation of escape from conformity, filled most of the page. Below the painting was a quote from Nietzsche: "The surest way to corrupt a youth is to instruct him to hold in higher esteem those who think alike than those who think differently." If you searched the entire page for a commercial message, you would find none. A line near the bottom read "Container

Corporation of America," and a company logo appeared as an afterthought to identify the procurer of these great ideas.

I was forewarned by an earlier interview I had with Procter & Gamble—the recruiter graded me high on ambition but failed me on my non-preppy appearance. He was a kind interviewer and offered advice. Apparently I had too much of Brooklyn in me, a touch too much of the immigrant. Though I didn't get the job, I was spared a worse fate.

F. Scott Fitzgerald described what happened to his father after he was fired by Procter & Gamble: "That morning he had gone out a comparatively young man, a man full of strength, full of confidence. He came home that evening an old man, a completely broken man . . . He was a failure the rest of his days."

At any rate, working myself up for a second Container Corporation of America interview I didn't consult Nietzsche before asking a barber to cut my hair. I also bought a suit at S. Klein on Union Square in Manhattan. The suit was fashioned to sell to organization men who knew they would have to sit at desks for long periods of time—it came with two pairs of slacks. It was gray flannel, too. The clothes, the haircut, the subdued style—I was coached to keep my expansive hand gestures modest—paid off.

Flown to Chicago to meet the vice president of manufacturing, I was dutifully impressed by his vast aspen-paneled office, large enough to house a platoon of soldiers. The style among executives, one that appealed to me, appeared to be so genteel as to suggest that money was not spoken here, at least not loudly. It looked like a good fit, and they hired me.

I became a management trainee, assigned to work with an industrial engineer whose job was to stand with a stopwatch and time the number of corrugated sheets that a laboring man could load onto a die-cut platen in a given period of time. The sheets were scored and cut one at a time.

The working man's skill was awesome. His arms flew in wide circles at eye level as he fed the die-cutter. His upper body swung with a ballet dancer's ease and grace in the follow-through motion of his arms. He could have been Rudolf Nureyev dancing with Margot Fonteyn in *Swan Lake*. I still remember how beautifully the operator could make the paperboard sheets fly, all day long.

What was I doing with the industrial engineer? I stood with a clipboard, trying to look informed while the engineer counted the number of sheets being cut in order to determine a man's capacity for work. The man was earning too much money in bonus, the engineer said. The quota might have to be adjusted higher. Today we have computers to micromanage us and do the industrial engineer's job. Productivity and efficiency are indeed helpful to keep consumer prices low, but the attempt to go further and further in pricing labor lower and lower can make widgets out of all of us, and deserves to be condemned.

A season passed unnoticed. I moved up the line of industrial command. Donna completed college. The Northwest, where I was discharged from active military service at Fort Lewis, lingered affectionately in our memory. I asked my company to transfer me to the West Coast. They declined, but Boeing hired me as a systems analyst and paid for our move to Seattle, and then trained me in COBOL computer coding to program inventory cycles. After some months Boeing promoted me to work as a market analyst, changing my employee badge from yellow (engineering) to orange (staff, management.) This was the era when companies had a contract with America, and trained their own US employees instead of getting special visas to import foreign workers. I was happy with Boeing, a fine company then, and a great company today. If I had a choice, I'd never fly in anything other than a Boeing commercial aircraft. But I was also young and restless, and all too aware that my youth was a perishable shelf-dated item. Without a family-inherited business or a professional livelihood to look forward to, I needed to spend my youth wisely. I inquired if the West Coast Container management might need my help now that I was on the West Coast, without them having had to pay for my move. I'd burned no bridges leaving them. They said come on back.

The folding-carton division hires me—think of Birds Eye frozen food packages. I like the company and my new management team: competent, eager at work, intelligent, and shimmering with polished surfaces, stylish offices, Eames chairs, designer office colors—the company was renowned for advanced design and graphic arts.

The office environment might have been similar to the offices at *Vogue* when Joan Didion worked there. But we were not in the fashion business as she was, nor did we deal in specialized patent-protected products like Apple and Microsoft do. We weren't like the company monopolizing the manufacture of indispensable, lifesaving EpiPens, who could raise the price five hundred percent to pay exorbitant executive salaries. We manufactured a high-quality product and sold it at a fair price, but others manufactured the same product and sold it for less. Aside from our design services, and efficient production methods, we had nothing unique to offer. In other words, we were in a commodity business and the cheapest price won.

How to survive? How to afford the Eames chairs and the corporate art collection eventually donated to the Smithsonian American Art Museum, in Washington DC, how to pay for the executive retreat in Aspen, Colorado, along with the aspen-paneled offices in Chicago and quarterly bonuses?

One of the easiest ways to beef up profits is to get chummy with your competitors, form a secret cartel and fix prices. A temptation we mostly avoided.

My responsibilities by then included production planning, purchasing, salaried clerks and accounting—a staff. I'm youngish as a manager, but not younger than the plant manager. Photographs show me at ease in my office. I'm wearing a casual shirt, my feet on the desk. Donna is visiting. She's pregnant, late term, but still teaching children in the Highline School District. We've bought a house in Fairwood Greens—the name describes it.

She leaves for home, and I go see my boss, the general manager. Usually he's utterly calm, but today he's looking distracted. Divisional management wants him to end the quarter with a profitable bang. He kneads his fingers gently, and approaches me with a tactical, rhetorical question: How could we make ourselves look a little better this month? Sales won't support it.

He knows the answer. I know the answer.

We can fudge a bit, smooth the edges, soften the rough spots, dance the numbers, massage them. How slippery is this slope? Just ask any investigative journalist, or read the business news most any week.

"What do you think?" the general manager asks smoothly. "Can you use your judgment?" My judgment is that as the newest youngish member of the management team, I would like to keep my job.

Before computers could provide precision tallies of work-in-progress, the amount of completed work had to be estimated. That's still true in construction today. No one actually counts the inches of wallboard installed: someone takes a guess and estimates the level of building completion so a bank can advance you more construction money.

Some long-running container manufacturing jobs take several months to complete, and the costs have to be apportioned across a span of time. My boss is asking me to guess high on job completion and guess low on the cost accrued. It's easy to push estimated costs from the current month to a future month, thus declaring—hurrah!—a larger operating profit in the current month. Thus we have what's called a "judgment" call, and judgment is the reason managers are managers—they're supposed to use their judgment, hopefully by not breaking the law. The numbers are balanced once a year.

In the world of petty accounting tricks and miscreant attitudes, this "smoothing the rough spots" or "massaging the numbers" didn't count for high crime in my view at the time, but it was petty mischief nonetheless. A venial sin if you're a Catholic, a traffic infraction and a fine if you're not, perhaps nothing more than a memoirist's misplaced chronology to smooth the narrative flow. The act of smoothing numbers, though, suggests deeper opportunities for misalignment.

Two Columbia University professors surveyed their alumni, expecting to prove the value of ethics courses in school. Forty percent of the graduates reported that they had been rewarded for taking some action they considered ethically troubling. Thirty-one percent said they were penalized for refusing to take an action that was ethically troubling. Some of the best-educated men and women in America end up doing what they know is wrong when, as one of them says, "push comes to shove."

Unfortunately, push comes to shove all too frequently in our lives. Though I ignored the subtly suggested advice, most times the numbers came out okay anyway. I cannot, however, claim a moral high ground, an Eliot Ness-like episode on TV, a successful *Mission: Impossible*, a dramatic breakout in my moral evolution, and a solid blow for decency. Instead I'm forced to think of Samuel Beckett more often than I would like. In *Waiting for Godot* he observes, "There's man ... blaming on his boots the faults of his feet."

One of the rewards of enthusiasm at work was a larger salary, enough to buy a sailboat. By then Donna and I had two children, though still in diapers. On the weekends, she and I would take them sailing, our ticket into the world of sea urchins, sand dollars, tide pools, and a group of friends that approximated our version of Virginia Woolf's Bloomsbury Group—architects, artists, professionals of several stripes and many ambitions, each of us questing, young, on the trail of this or that next thing. With our babies afoot, we're seekers, fielding ambition, desire, and organizing entertainment with beachside picnics and oyster bakes in the San Juans. This surplus of the good life came with watercolor painting expeditions, egg rolls on Easter Sunday and a marinated cooked goose at a communal table large enough to feed many. All of it was wonderful, including the goose, but none of it taught me how to be a master sailor.

Whenever we went sailing our worries receded as we watched the bow cleaving through curling waves of iridescent plankton-filled water. My mind could run free from the uncertainties of fate, the vagaries of chance, and the requirement to choose wisely between life's many paths. That day, though, I chose badly to go sailing. The storm of the century crossed the Pacific to take down Hood Canal Bridge.

The children were terrified in the cabin below. Our Irish Setter and the wind were both howling. The waves so huge, their cresting white tips shooting needle-like spray.

It was a small sailboat. There was nothing wrong with the motor, or the hull, or the depth sounder, the mast, the sails, the wind vane, the two-way radio, the dinghy, or the Danforth anchor. All the shortcomings belonged to the skipper—me—and my poor judgment. What possessed me to go sailing that day with two children in diapers on board?

We were wearing life vests, but what good would that have done if we violently capsized? And there was another danger—safety was farther from the coast, out at sea, but the winds had pushed us dangerously close to shore. Donna took the helm to keep the bow pointed into the wind as I worked my way forward, hand over hand to shorten the main-sail and keep the wind from running us aground. I reefed the mainsail to the boom and left a small triangle of sail for stability.

The depth sounder sounded an alarm. We were about to run aground. I grabbed at stanchions and cabin handholds to pull myself to the bow, and then dropped the anchor. The line jerked across my leather-gloved hands. The shore kept getting closer, the alarm louder. I cleated the anchor line's bitter end and felt helpless from then on, disaster imminent, the shoreline ominously close.

In that moment I caught Donna's eye, and saw our death unfolding, our children lost. Our yellow storm gear illuminated us, the orange life vests padded us. Her woolen cap was soaked, her face sea-wet but without fear, resigned. So this was how it would end. We were still young, the children not having lived. It seemed so suddenly quiet, even though the storm was raging. The shattering sky was blown apart by cumulus cloud hammers darkening. The uncertainty of life was ending, the challenges, the work, the beauty. We were at peace, together.

Just then the anchor caught the seabed. The wind roared, the sail blew out and the boom tipped into the sea. The boat rocked wildly, yanked at the anchor, tugged sideways, and then steadied, swinging its bow tight into oncoming winds. The anchor held. We bobbed safely off-shore. The children were safe.

A youth standing at the dock of a nearby motel had witnessed our distress, bravely rowed out, and took the children ashore. He then returned for us and our dog. We booked a room and the children were soon asleep. The refreshment cooler held wine. We opened the bottle and filled our glasses. Seated in front of a window we watched the winds hurling water at us, but our room, our lives felt steady.

"I didn't want to die before the children were grown," Donna said.

We ignored the illogical: the children would have died, too.

"I put you at risk," I said.

Saved from imminent disaster we felt reborn, alive. We made love as though we expected to die. We made love to save our lives, abandoning ourselves to each other. In the morning it was eerily calm.

Clarity often comes after the storm, not before. Back at work Monday, I questioned every aspect of my misplaced eagerness to sail. Is this how decisions are made on the highest government levels? The unprovoked second war on Iraq was sold to us as a "slam dunk" that would destroy the never-found weapons of mass destruction, and be over in sixty days. Such executive follies are best committed by confident men and women. I didn't realize I was such myself. What possessed me to risk the lives of my wife and children by sailing that day?

Soon after my sailing debacle a divisional executive, Mr. Harris Tweed, a privileged corporate mandarin who enjoyed good press in *Fortune* magazine and lived in a mansion, came visiting. One of the duties of Mr. Tweed was to scour the various plants under his jurisdiction and evaluate the executives, especially members of the junior class like me who might be promoted to divisional in California or headquarters in Chicago.

"Hear! Hear!" Mr. Tweed said, crowning my general manager's comment on a point now long forgotten as we dined at the upscale Canlis restaurant above the sparkling mirage-like evening lights of Lake Union. I was looking appropriately executive, articulate and knowledgeable, eager to take on larger responsibilities. But I didn't want to leave Seattle, and the company's local opportunities were limited.

"You'll never *belong* to this group," Donna whispered.

Second insight, I suppose. I'm the Brooklyn kid who graduated City College of New York, proudly described by some as "the poor man's Harvard." I loved the opportunity, the teachers. Whatever my pride in modest college achievement, the school is not the socially privileged place that Yale, Harvard, Princeton or Stanford are. Some have called it The Little Red Schoolhouse, hoping to strangle the humanist social values for which it is well known.

Nonetheless, I'm a former soda jerk. Ever-restless, I wanted to move beyond the corporate plateau I'd reached. Besides, not all was going well with my purveyor of Great Ideas of Western Man. Mr. Harris Tweed would soon be sentenced to jail for collaborating in a price-fixing scheme. It was time for me to hit the road. Time to attempt self-employment.

18

THE BUSINESS DONNA AND I HAVE CHOSEN TO LAUNCH, A franchised floor-covering store, is as humdrum as any you can enter with zero retailing skills, limited business knowledge, and zero capital. The franchise's major attraction was the financing provided. We launched our business with nearly one hundred percent borrowed money. In the place of the cash that we didn't have, we contributed sweat capital. Sweat capital is also *fear* capital—a friendly fear, a cautioning fear. It sticks to your skin, doesn't wash off in the shower.

I get to work at seven in the morning to organize the carpet installers. They leave to install carpet across the city. A few shoppers wander in during morning hours. I'm alert to each walk-in. We're into big-ticket sales—carpeting the living room, dining room, and hall, sometimes two or three additional bedrooms included.

The number of customers was never large, but all you needed was one good sale each day to make your day. Donna joins me by mid-morning to attend to the paperwork. She has the quick movements of someone always behind schedule, running a race of obscure beginnings. Our children are still young enough to be kept in a playpen inside the office. She's given up teaching to help in the business. She does the office work and comes with me on sales calls in the evening when a babysitter is available. We hire a salesman but keep working through the day, catching a bite to eat whenever we can. The daily pattern is slow, but on our three-day sale events the pace was hectic.

Even after we hire a second salesman, we work every day, every three-day holiday, on call or at work 24/7, twelve months a year. I'm the chief salesman. Whenever we take a week off, sales plummet. We see our friends at large companies, or in the professions, taking off on vacations, sabbaticals, sometimes a month at a time, sometimes longer. We can't budge, we can't leave, we can't get free from work. You turn your back on a startup business and it typically cascades downward. Night enters our lives.

"I need a life," Donna says.

"I need you."

"A garden."

"Talk to me."

There's darkness afoot in our world. Can we leave the house of work we've built? Can we alter the contours of our lives? Do we even have a *self* anymore? Other youngish couples have tried similar retail ventures and learning what we were learning, abandoned them quickly. We persist nonetheless.

Our children grow older. They can now safely play on the carpet rolls, slide off the waterfall carpet displays. They're happy and carefree. We suspect that life is brutal. That it can pounce on you, empty you, erase you. We hope that our children can be as happy in later life as they seem to be now.

The business turns out to be a modest success, though we're feeling scruffy from the effort. We speculate that with only one store we'll never get beyond a hand-to-mouth existence. I persuade a banker to lend us the construction financing and a commercial mortgage to build a second store, a freestanding building in a small town within the Seattle metro area. We build the second store, and keep the vacant land that one day would tempt Bollinger. We're looking to quell our uneasiness, but we're actually doubling down on our anxiety.

The town where we locate the second store has a population less than forty thousand people. There are many apartments and a few senior housing developments. There are also many, many churches. You'll find the Rotary here; Elks and Lions are in town, the Chamber of Commerce. Good people live here, clerks, mechanics, retirees, a few professionals but mostly working-class people. Their houses are built on old farmland. Their children are healthy. A picture of middle-Middle America. The city throbs along a ganglia of retail strips with a large regional shopping mall at its head. The big event in town is the mall.

As people moved into the county, as Boeing manufacturing expanded at nearby Paine Field and small industries boomed, the value of the land next to the store we built, increased. Like a well-fed steer it became prime, a triple-A location in the argot of real-estate salesmen.

The region's economy changed, too. Unlike the time we moved to Seattle, when unemployment skyrocketed and some wag put up a billboard, "Will the last person leaving turn out the lights?" Seattle was now growing. Tech was booming. Boeing talked of a five-year backlog, nearly every fast-food store displayed prominent "now hiring" signs. The multiplex movies had arrived to keep us entertained.

It's our turn on the wheel of fortune. Or so we think. Our friends' lives start unraveling around us, disintegrating in slow motion. The bloom of youth fades. Not all ambitions and efforts are rewarded, despite the effort and talent applied. Too much examining has been going on in the past decade. Defects, defaults, short measures, unmet promises accumulate in the privately held books of complaint. Partners examining each other were coming up short on what they had imagined the future should have delivered.

An acquaintance says his soon-to-be-ex-wife is insane. He's plotting to take control of the properties and children they've accumulated together. A friend dies under strange circumstances in a locked room plastered with gay porn. Friends escape into drugs and alcohol and affairs. A man we hire, extremely bright, charming, and well-spoken, a former accountant who wanted a break from his profession and took a sales job with us, decides he's had enough of family life, enough of his two children and a registered nurse for a wife, enough of the grind, the morning traffic and the going-home traffic. He departs with an underage girlfriend to Guatemala. No fierce family fights for him. No divorce. No windup, no denouement, nothing about epiphanies. The post-youth disillusionment has set in. We bob and weave among the human losses.

19

THE YEARS COME AND GO, SEVERAL BUSINESSES COME AND go, and I find myself sitting in Bollinger's Cadillac dealership office. We've been meeting on and off, hide and seek, touch and go for over a year. He wants to bet his future on the new Lexus. To win a franchise he must have a building to occupy by September 1, 1989. This is the year the Berlin Wall comes down; the year Chinese students are massacred in Tiananmen Square, the year of the Velvet Revolution, the year Daw Aung San Suu Kyi, the leader of Myanmar's democracy movement, is arrested (she'll spend fifteen years under arrest), and the year the playwright Samuel Beckett dies.

Bollinger is looking to rearrange the paperwork on his desk. We've paused in a moment of uncertainty between us. The pictures of his children are on the credenza behind him. We might be near the same height, but the couch on which I'm sitting places me a foot lower. Competing egos aside, the former Marine officer and former Army draftee are now communicants, breaking business bread together. He tells me that Cadillac buyers were once a loyal V8 bunch faithful to the memory of fins and big chrome, and Fleetwood models so stretched that the Cadillac emblem on the front of the hood looked to be a football field's distance from the steering wheel.

"My best customers are dying," Bollinger says.

GM designers had taken a generational nap.

The forward-looking company that had created the popular Futurama exhibit at the 1939 World's Fair, a vision of utopia and consumer abundance, had predicted that GM would dominate an auto industry that would have thirty-eight million cars on the road by 1960. They underestimated. There were twice as many cars on the road by 1960, and GM dominated the market. Such success can invite complacency. By the late '80s many older lifelong Cadillac buyers were hanging up their holsters, unsaddling their broncos, fighting macular degeneration, turning in their driver's licenses, and booking gourmet cruises to sail off into the sunset. The wealthy among them might have a 1959 Cadillac Eldorado Biarritz worth a cool $250,000 sitting in their garage, but younger buyers were bypassing Caddy nostalgia to find snap and sizzle among competing brands.

The tepid rate of design change in the Cadillac division troubled Bollinger, which was why he was looking to win another car franchise. (The past keeps repeating itself every generation. In late 2014, to refresh its design and marketing energy, Cadillac moves its marketing division from Detroit to the Soho district in Manhattan.)

What did I know about cars to meet Bollinger's challenge? I've read *Unsafe at Any Speed* by Ralph Nader. I drove a car with eighty thousand miles on it. If someone mentioned valves, I was more inclined to think of the heart than a car engine. I did know that Datsun had morphed into Nissan. (I owned one.) I knew that the 240Z, the "Z" car, a zippy two-door sports car unleashed a frenzy of consumer happiness among American car buyers in 1969. I understood that Japanese products were valued for utility, reliability, and low prices. No one imagined they could build a car to compete with Mercedes-Benz or BMW.

In the late '80s I've not heard of the car Bollinger is pitching to me. His car lot and showroom display many shiny new cars. What isn't American made is British. What's missing from the floor is anything remotely Japanese. Donna tells me that aside deep-sea pearls found off the coast of Japan that she's used in crafting jewelry, no other luxury Japanese products, other than sushi, come to mind.

"A Japanese luxury car," he says to catch my attention. He adjusts his large frame to sit comfortably, and then he amends his statement. "We haven't seen the car yet, and we don't have the car pricing. Lower-priced, though."

My experience with auto dealers isn't deep or extensive. When I'm feeling literary, I might look up John Updike's Rabbit Angstrom; otherwise I think of the hustling man on TV speed talking, explaining why I should buy a car this weekend because the sale ends at ten p.m. Sunday and I'll never ever again see such a *fantastic* deal that'll save me thousands of dollars.

Similar ads ran every year, every month.

Bollinger is giving me another view. He doesn't look like a man who likes to shout. He defies the TV-sponsored clichés I've associated with car dealers. He is earnest and levelheaded, and trained as a Marine officer. He doesn't match the cartoonish images shown on TV.

His office on the mezzanine level has a clear view of the showroom below. It's a busy day with high customer traffic, and the salesmen are more attentive than bored. In 2014 *Automotive News* would report that forty-one percent of luxury-auto salespeople quit each year, and a stunning seventy-four percent of non-luxury auto salespeople quit every year. I try to imagine what's it like to deal with such sales anxiety, always seeking, here today and poor tomorrow, looking for the next better opportunity.

In the evening I'll say to Donna, *Here's what he wants ...*

We had gone to see Arthur Miller's *Death of a Salesman* soon after I graduated City College. The desperation portrayed in that American masterpiece convinced me that I'd never work as a salesman. As the evidence in this memoir suggests, I might have made the wrong call about my participation in sales. But that early conviction aimed me toward manufacturing management, and then toward administration. On each level of modest success, I learned that avoiding sales—which one can define as asserting oneself and one's resources in a favorable light—wasn't a good idea.

Turning away from the showroom overlook, I notice a three-foot-tall bronze depicting a mounted cowboy. The cowboy looks vaguely familiar. A replica of a Frederic Remington work? The artist said: "I never intend to do any great amount of labor. I have but one short life and do not aspire to wealth or fame in a degree which could only be obtained by an extraordinary effort on my part." I'm also reminded that William Blake, though pinched by poverty, refused to confine himself to "the mere drudgery of business."

That sentiment is shared by many artists.

But then I look closer. It's not a knockoff Remington. It's actually John Wayne with a Winchester, tall and lean, strong chin, woodcut features, riding a bucking bronco. An art historian might describe the sinewy interplay of bronco energy and male coolness as Cowboy Mannerism. Wayne looks as if he'd been riding from the age of ten, probably wearing a plaid-checkered Western shirt, tooled leather boots and a felt cowboy hat. He didn't much like horses, though. The Duke put it this way: "I don't get on a horse unless they pay me."

Born in Iowa, John Wayne started his life as Marion Robert Morrison, and later became known as Duke Morrison. I'm sympathetic toward such naming reinventions. I tried several and adopted Holland Kane as a pseudonym for the novels I've written. My given name, Gediminas, which in its diminutive Lithuanian form is Gedukas, can be shortened to Dukas, and then further simplified in English to Duke. (A name Donna loathed.) At the point of extreme simplification, I've lopped off the "G" from Gediminas, embraced "Ed" that followed, and dropped the remainder to identify myself as Ed. Friends appreciate the simpler tag. But on my credit cards, driver's license, naturalization document, and Army discharge papers, Gediminas remains.

That aside, John Wayne chose a name he made famous. Clearly, Bollinger would like some fame too. But the moment I hear what I'm being offered by him, my impulse is to get up and walk away. I can almost hear John Wayne drawl, but it's Bollinger who's speaking, "I don't want to say this …"

He looks away without saying it.

How long have we been bickering? If it's not one thing, it's another. Which is a good thing. The ball is in play. We must have something going, but neither one of us knows for sure.

I'm handed a document that his lawyer has drafted. I think I've seen this before, or something similar. Or heard something like it. I'm looking at a page that reads like a replay of a tedious TV segment I might have seen before. A complex risk-weighing transaction often teeters between the medieval and the postmodern. Today it's medieval, an addendum standoff, a joust of irreconcilable paragraphs.

"You're not even sure you'll get the Lexus franchise," I say.

"I'm almost sure, Ed … But I don't have a guarantee."

He's more than half sure, maybe three-quarters sure that he'll win a franchise. Each new assessment of his winning ability rises higher than the last assessment. A silent unseen person sits at our conference table: the Lexus division. He must first show Toyota—at the time the largest auto company in the world—that he owns, or has secured by way of contract, a piece of land on which he can build a Lexus building designed by the auto manufacturer on a site Lexus approves. Toyota won't give him the franchise until he has everything lined up. Without the Lexus franchise, no bank will lend him the rest of the money he needs for his startup. He's facing a typical business-launch problem. No one wants to bet on you unless you're already a winner. A situation most unpublished writers face.

"I hope I'll get the franchise," he says, his trademark optimism sparkling. He could be thinking of the competing dealers looking to nail down a Lexus franchise. Most would have no difficulty raising the cash to buy five acres, let alone two acres from me. We're not making much headway today. Despite our earlier agreement to agree, the meeting winds down without progress.

20

OLLINGER'S GENERAL MANAGER, MIKE LANE, JOINS US AT our next meeting. We're expecting Lexus executives to arrive from L.A. The three of us are up for inspection by Japanese officials. They're late. Traffic, we're told, a flight delayed, but we don't know for sure, and we're edgy.

Mike's hair is close cut, salt and pepper, meticulously groomed. His words are measured in a slow cadence. Like Bollinger, he strikes me as a good man to work for, willing to listen. I've been observing him more closely. They've been together a while. Mike has earned recognition outside the dealership and had been offered an opportunity to buy a GM franchise in a small town but chose to stay, hoping that together they might find a better and larger opportunity still.

He adds an occasional verbal gesture at the end of a sentence that echoes Bollinger's voice, sometimes made obvious when he uses the same turns of speech or retells a joke once told by Bollinger.

At this meeting we're all wearing suits. My shoes are shined. Our ties are subdued. We wear the costume of the play we're performing, *THE SUITS*—and today we're performing for our Japanese overlords.

We chat to pass the time.

"What are you going to do if you can't sell enough cars?" I ask.

"We've been thinking about that," Mike acknowledges. "A good used-car operation could absorb a lot of overhead." The gross margins on clean late-model used cars are better than the margins on new cars. The sale of an extended warranty, accessories, and the markup on financing will bring in more money. "I'm going to build up the service department by hiring the best mechanics in the area, maybe someone with a following." They ask me if I know of anyone to recommend. I've recently brought my old car to Auto Recyclers to have it fitted with a junked wrecking-yard transmission, not the best reference to give to a luxury-car dealer. I say that I don't know anyone.

Bollinger is not so easily habituated to thrift as I am. He likes the gold flourish. His wife won't be seen without a designer bag. Socially helpful contributions to the Seattle Symphony, along with his steady and substantial support of the Washington State Cougars football team is expensive. Which is why I've continued to park my car out on the street rather than driving it onto Bollinger's lot. The dull exterior would look all the worse surrounded by an acre of sparkling new cars, brilliant with the promise of ownership.

"We know that the service business is going to be tough," Mike Lane says. "A new high-quality model like the one we expect from Lexus won't support it alone." It turns out that about half the new-car dealerships in the United States wouldn't earn a profit without a service department. He gives me a card stamped in silver and engraved, "Cadillac Master Manager." A point of pride, as it should be. We master what pleases us and often find that our mastery is never enough. Once I presumed to be a master of business administration. I learned otherwise. I'm thinking I might apply to a *Master of Fine Arts* program in search of another elusive mastery.

A call from the receptionist interrupts us. Bollinger goes to the showroom to meet the Lexus executives and a man from Saatchi & Saatchi, an international advertising firm hired by Lexus. They come upstairs. The Lexus zone manager introduces us to a mysterious Japanese executive whose title I fail to catch. He wears a light sport coat, dark brown slacks. He speaks infrequently and tries to smile and finds it painful as if troubled by a sensitive tooth. In automotive parlance, he's the hood ornament. He doesn't do much but you don't travel without him.

They've brought pictures of the proposed car, racy line drawings, a futuristic look on glossy paper. I study it, unable to judge its appeal. It looks great on paper, in pictures. Bollinger catches my ambivalence. "We don't know how it's going to look exactly." Part of the marketing strategy is to drape the car in mystery. "No one has seen the car except Roger Penske." Penske is an auto-industry icon, a racecar driver, a racing team leader, smart, energetic, audacious, industrious, a man with foresight who has trained all his life to be a winner. We're looking to someone with national industry clout to give us guidance. "He's absolutely sold on the car. He says he hasn't driven anything like it."

I feel encouraged. I want to be encouraged.

Off to the side, I have a few words with the American Lexus executive. "The Japanese ask very good questions," he tells me, "They listen, they really listen." There's a touch of awe in his tone. Americans, we don't like to listen; we like to talk. The exec and I puzzle over the changes.

Toyota motor cars are astonishingly good. Surely the Lexus is a marvel, three hundred patents in all. Credit should be given to the Japanese, but this credit, like the credit we offer a tradesman for his mercantile skills, an engineer for designing bridges to hold up, or the craftsman for his attention to detail, though laudable and useful, isn't enough to build our nation.

As Eleanor Roosevelt argued: "America is not a pile of goods, more luxury, more comforts, a better telephone system, a greater number of cars. America is a dream of greater justice, and opportunity for the average man and, if we can not obtain it, all our achievements amount to nothing."

The Japanese executive wants to see the site. I know he must. Without his okay, nothing happens. Lexus must approve the site, the lease, the building plans, the construction, the final result—and only then will they grant the permanent Lexus franchise to Bollinger. It's not just that they have a carrot to entice him. They can bludgeon him with a club. I'm a smile away from receiving a sorrowful call filled with regret. *Good try, Ed. It's just not going to work. Sorry.* And he would be sorry, and sincere.

We split into a three-car caravan. I'm in a car with one of the Lexus executives driving. I'm showing him a longer route past the new Acura dealership not far from the proposed Lexus site. I want to be sure they know that Ford, Honda, Toyota, Nissan and Volvo dealerships along Highway 99 are located close. Car dealerships experience more customer traffic, and sales, if they're close to each other. "Auto row," I say. I'm a tour guide adding local color. I report that Honeywell is moving in, software companies growing, Boeing expanding. Though the average income of families living cheek by jowl to the site is low, I want them to understand that prospering, high-salaried people live nearby. I mention the expensive, three- and four-car garage homes along the bluffs overlooking the Puget Sound. I want them to like the site. I want them to know that customers will drive miles to get to an easily accessible auto row site.

My enthusiasm aside, the highway strip looks dreary today. The long grass on the ground hasn't dried out from a week of rain. Sunshine breaks loose from dense clouds as we arrive. The sun makes the site look larger. My long-lapsed faith blossoms to thank God for the sun and the golden Scotch broom patches that have burst into bloom.

We park along the curb. No one wants to walk the perimeter through the soggy muck and weeds. Our shoes, polished, gleaming, keep us rooted to the sidewalk. The homeless man won't have our company today. No one mentions the existing Abbey Carpet building crowding the site. Bollinger queries the assembled executives silently. A slight motion of his head signals his own satisfaction. All eyes are on the silent Japanese executive. He nods. We smile.

21

ENCOURAGED BY OUR ADVANCING CAR PALACE NEGOTIATIONS, Donna and I grab our children for a drive to the picturesque town of La Conner, once a fishing village, now Tom Robbins' town, author of *Even Cowgirls Get the Blues*.

It's a rural country road. Fields of pink and red, magenta and gold, and ivory tulips come into view. Pacific and San Juan breezes have blown away the haze. The children are excited to get out among the flowers. The sky is crystal pale and we're talking about a perfect Sunday. I pull over to the side of the road. The children scamper out. We yell at them to keep to the path as they run toward the flowers. Donna sits in the car.

"Walk with me?" I ask.

Our hands touch. "All I need are flowers," she says.

"All I need is you."

"That's almost like being in love."

Writers offer many observations about marriage. One describes it as "institutionalized dishonesty," "a cult of sentimentality and sur-faces." Another offers this nugget attributed to Virginia Woolf, "I loathe marriage. I hate its smugness, its safety, its compromise ..." Could Virginia Woolf have been talking about herself and her devoted husband Leonard? I'm not an academic, my research skills are limited. But if that quote is accurate, it's probably taken out of context.

Eva Illouz explores and analyzes the love market in her book *Why Love Hurts*, offering much-needed scholarship. She questions our high expectations, inspects the low results as we shop in a romance bazaar, a place to buy and sell love, and consume sex, with little hope that anything will last, except the constant plotting and dodging and weaving in the pursuit of the most effective romantic and sexual way to spread one's genes.

For that we need sex. In her breathtaking memoir, *Future Sex*, Emily Witt describes today's roustabout freedom to enjoy sex unfettered by tradition. Her exploration of the bold and the sensually tremulous in her own life offers insight into the alternative ways others experience their sexual lives. Humane and perceptive and forthright in her observations, Witt concedes that a woman's search for satisfaction can remain unsatisfied. She writes: "Love is rare, and it is frequently unreciprocated."

At home, Donna runs a finger across the seductive book jacket. "Every boy's dream?" she asks. The orange-tinted photograph suggests a woman's pleasure made proper for public display by a blue circle that hides intimacy but announces sex in the title.

"They call it polyamory now. Polyfidelity? Something like that," I say.

"A theme and variation on sexual practices in the '60s and '70s?"

"The tune hasn't changed."

"The same old song—open marriage."

"Men seem to prefer it more than women do. But the bottomless variety of internet dating must satisfy many."

"Sounds sexhausting."

Serial love, a dance of many doubts and attractions, remains powerful and wonderful. Larry King forgot about dating and married eight times, though only to seven women. Elizabeth Taylor also married eight times; famously, she married Richard Burton twice.

But if love is a sport, as some claim it is, one could say that the goalposts keep shifting as emotions weigh on the years of our youth. Bobbing in this sea of contradictions, Donna and I are sympathetic to love, love at first sight if you're lucky, even elusive lasting love. There are corridors of my mind where her steps echo; her voice carries when nothing is said.

Everyone builds their own opinion of what makes a marriage work. There are times when Donna is exasperated that I had not heard her, perhaps not even listened. "I don't want to occupy the suburbs of your mind," she says. "I'm center city, I'm downtown." And so she is.

Nevertheless, the critic Shulamith Firestone declares that love "is the pivot of women's oppression."

Writers come up with the most troubling things to write about. We're superbly self-licensed to explore the uncertainties in our lives, and then rail and rouse and riot with words aimed at others. Words are war. Life is fragile. Hope decays quickly. I'm working to cast my lot among writers, exploring passages, transitions, even scenes from a marriage.

Writing can be a high-wire act. One slip can trip you up. A false step might damn you. A longer piece might expel you from polite society. Nevertheless, I'm looking to feel whatever writers feel when they create lives on the page, offering excitement, mystery, heart songs, conflict, news and opinion, perhaps even love.

The writer in me attempts to make sense of marriage. Sex and desire aside, why do many of us make, and work toward, a lifelong commitment in marriage? Until death do us part? We know the odds. We see the wonderful variety of exciting and talented people who could have partnered with us. It's frequently easier to let go, to start fresh, to abandon the marital field in favor of next engaging romantic moment.

Why did Donna choose not to do it? She's had plenty of opportunities to abandon our marriage. With good-looking men. More powerful, more talented than me. What's kept us together? Are we more Lithuanian than American? Our families were destroyed by the Soviets. We could never go home again. Our homelessness turned us inward, made us more observant, more introspective, and gave us more of each other to ourselves.

Marriage can be like two pebbles confined under a trickle of water that grinds both into sand; or two trees planted too closely together pushing each other out of shape, mutually supportive, mutually distortive. Paintings by Marc Chagall give another picture of marriage. Amid the blues of a late afternoon sky, over a smudge or two of red in a field of white, men and women float about, ethereal, some of them holding hands, some a bit spooky and upside down.

Donna and I have been upside down, too, but we have tenure of sorts with each other, room to commit mistakes, omissions, missed connections; every word isn't recorded, or questioned and cross-examined. We have privacy with each other, and spaces of solitude even when we're together. We didn't make a brilliant marriage. We fell in love and remained loving.

We have friends, married and partnered, who are into thoroughly examined relationships. They will tease every nugget, weigh every ounce, parse every word to grow seeds of alienation, seeds of disappointment, regret for the time wasted with an unsuitable partner, opportunities lost, all listed in their private journals of discontent. Socrates would be appalled by the misuse of his famous observation that an unexamined life is not worth living.

Donna and I have different tastes, attitudes, and hopes—a friend has compared us to the gorgeously mated Eclectus parrot pair. The male is utterly green with a touch of turquoise, the female feathered in regal red and a touch of purple. These are not birds of a feather. Admired alone, each bird looks so different, so individualized, that few would ever guess they belong to the same species. I would like to think that our marriage is perhaps like that of the beautifully strange birds. It's also no mere fluke, no lucky run—accidents don't take so many years to mature. And all those years to examine? No mere hello, no quick goodbye. We could have fallen a dozen times. And yet ...

Aside from nesting together we're also under fire from larger forces. Our actions are quickened by the need to survive, our emotions heightened by our closeness to failure. Because we have fought through so many ventures together, none of them great, and survived the skirmishes—random wins, many losses—our togetherness is not an abstract concept.

Chagall isn't fashionable today. His pictures allow you to wander—moments of confusion follow one another without embarrassment. Physical perfection is reassuringly absent. He paints a generous democratic Walt Whitmanesque canvas. There's no belligerence behind the brushstrokes, no perfection of forms, no ramparts to mount and defend, no firing squad to avoid, and pretension is absent. So you might want to forgive him for painting doves. He's not offering the sensual history of sex, or a narrative describing evolution. The poetics of an occasional Hallmark card shouldn't wither anyone's intellect, unless there's not much intellect worth withering.

I respect intellectuals who have grave doubts about lasting relationships. They've failed many. Few of us believe we're wired for monogamy. The energy aimed at biodiversity can make us fools in bed. Culture, though, is often the collar. Donna, unwilling to give ground in this feminist marital debate, pokes at the critics of marriage, and buys me a gift—a small wall hanging embroidered in a Western homestead style that reads: *Home Sweet Home~~Never Stop Fucking Me.*

22

E. M. FORSTER NOTED THAT THE MIDDLE CLASS IS MARKED BY "solidity, caution, integrity, efficiency. Lack of imagination, hypocrisy." If some of that might be true, he didn't go far enough to mention that such character traits are widely applied to the rich and poor alike. The middle class, more than other classes, has a capacity for work unseen before, driven by ambition to gain something better in life than it has inherited, while clinging to a cliff that threatens every foothold above the abyss of poverty.

The middle class also tends to dream big. Hopes run wide for this or that Lotto-like commercial breakthrough, a change in one's life. Frank and April Wheeler, the archetypal American characters masterfully created by Richard Yates in *Revolutionary Road* and let loose to smash themselves against fate, keep cropping up in my mind as examples of hope explored, and desire denied. Frank, captive to Western ideas of authenticity, is looking to "find himself" by moving to Paris, while April, criticized for her acting in a local theater production, seeks escape from the roles a woman performs in suburban acts—they're both planning a jailbreak from the conventions that rule their lives.

Yates's novel engaged my imagination near the beginning of the car palace negotiations. It was the year I attended a Centrum workshop at Port Townsend taught by the novelist Margaret Atwood. She arranged us into editorial committees tasked with the job of deciding if we wanted to publish the prose of the participants attending. If I recall the workshop correctly, nothing was published. No one liked anyone's writing.

My classmates and I are writers without portfolios, without editors, without published books, without media connections, without the academic careers and the MFA programs that have served many talented writers who turn to teaching because they can't earn a living writing. As beginners in a writing workshop, we are mostly admiring pawns, a book-buying market for the established writers teaching the classes. Some teachers are exceptional, many are helpful, a few are terrible beyond redemption.

Atwood, an excellent teacher, a treasured writer, is on to the game and admits that teaching a writing class is better than waitressing which is how she supported herself while writing her first books. The impression I retain is that teaching isn't much better than waitressing. At any rate, she chooses not to teach craft but to show us the realities of publishing, which is why we've been organized into editorial committees, three or four of us to a group, all the better to give us anonymity as we snipe at each other's contributions.

Several of the pieces deal with family members, a difficult subject.

Geoffrey Wolff competently dissects his father in *The Duke of Deception* with his usual, admirable, delicate skill. The Duke of the title is governed by energy that fuels many promoters, marketers, and salespeople—a wild-eyed optimism that can be imaginative, outrageous, sometimes tawdry, bombastic, and is often successful.

Parents often come up short in children's recollections. But as subjects, we're in the forefront of a memoir industry. Frank Conroy, teaching another class I attended, helped launch the modern memoir genre with his book *Stop-Time*. The Wolff brothers, Geoffrey and Tobias, separated when young, have successfully mined a long stretch of sketchy parenting. Geoffrey pursuing his father, and Tobias following in his celebrated brother's footsteps by scrutinizing their mother. Parents are easy targets. Sitting ducks, so to speak. Unsentimental psychological investigations and middle-class sentimentality seem to be well mated. Though I'm a fan of such books, I'm reminded again of Virginia Woolf's observation that nonfiction is a poor variant of fiction.

John McPhee, who teaches a course he's reluctantly named Creative Nonfiction has tackled the awkward juxtaposition of the words "creative" and "nonfiction" by separating the conjoined creature into:

(a) the creative part—your choice of subject, scene, dialogue, diction, detail and scope, blended with a mix of observation, opinion and description that can be ornery or beautiful, insightful or nitwitted. The style and cadences of speech might embrace or reject metaphor, analogy, allegory, perhaps dabble in symbolism of one kind or another, all of it patterned by punctuation that may clarify, imply, suggest. This fertile selection, if it works well, will evoke a mood, a tone, a register to enliven characters. It becomes your sound on paper, your literary voice.

And,

(b) the nonfiction part—what we perceive as facts.

Some of us writing have to study to learn this, others are gifted by nature. I've run out of shelf space for all the good books voicing many opinions. Some are stacked in vertical columns against the brick of an unused fireplace, among them several books by Judith Seabrook, a skillful writer and a strident, doctrinaire teacher that I'm fated to meet.

The distinguished critic Elaine Showalter explains in *Teaching Literature* that twelve or so students cooped up with a teacher every week for a semester can cause the teacher much anxiety. I can report that there's as much student anxiety as teacher anxiety. I sat eight to twelve feet away from Seabrook, pinned down in a captive audience of fellow students. Battered by her sharp nasal voice, we caught her gestures, the dismissive motions, as we listened to cringe-worthy criticisms aimed at the conduct of men. Yet, there's the other part—Seabrook has written thoughtfully and with sensitivity about her own youthful trials, rejections and exclusions—a pain that still lurks in the pores of her skin.

I'll have a private lunch with her. Just the two of us, teacher and student. I get to pay. She'll mention a relationship in the intermediate stage that she says with confidence "won't last." She's sure of it. The "situation" is conditional, she says, weighed on a quid pro quo. She has a Manichean certainty, a Machiavellian plan to jump ship at the next best moment.

Donna and I are naïve by comparison, inexperienced. I'm reminded of a sailing vessel we once named *Footloose* to suggest freedom. *Footloose* had a dinghy named *Fancy Free*. To get where we wished to go, sailing often required lots of zigzagging (tacking) to catch the wind. Occasionally we sailed downwind, untroubled. The downwind leg, though, never lasted as long as we wanted. We had to keep working the sails, adjusting them this way and that way. Not infrequently we had to change course to avoid rocks and shoals. But most of the dangers were marked by navigation buoys.

Sailing in a sea of people is more challenging. It's not as easy to see the obstacles you need to avoid. As luck would have it, we hit a shoal while on board an airplane preparing to take off. Seabrook boards the plane. Most of the overhead bins are shut. She hustles to the back of the crowded plane. There is an empty aisle seat next to Donna. I wave. Seabrook plunks down and sighs. Soon we're aloft and making small talk. Donna, brimming with her usual, unsuspecting good cheer, asks if Betty Friedan is as intimidating in person as some in the press were then reporting. *"You* would be intimidated," Seabrook declares with the force of a viper about to strike. Her eyes flash like fangs. Where did the venom come from? Donna is startled. I am too. Seabrook hadn't met Donna before.

Roused to voice my own biases I see Seabrook's mind damaged beyond kindness by Marxist flirtations. An intellectual brimming with derision for the middle class. (To which she also belongs.) But Seabrook never had to labor with her hands, manage a tribe, work at a mill, burden a mortgage, bear and protect children. She had, in fact, never been poor. She had never been a DP—a Displaced Person. Her parents never had to look for food scraps to feed her as Donna's did. This freedom from want, apparently, gave her licenses to brag that she could easily ignore the death of hundreds of thousands of strangers if she could just keep the people on her urban island to herself. The luminous critic Alfred Kazin, author of the deeply felt, sensually evocative, *A Walker in the City,* would say that Seabrook suffers from a "fatal want of generosity."

As children, Donna and I were dazzled by the height of American skyscrapers. The earflaps on my winter cap were turned halfway toward my nose as I disembarked the SS *America* with my parents. The cultural critic Leslie Fiedler explains, "to be an American (unlike being English or French or whatever) is precisely to *imagine* a destiny rather than inherit one; since we have always been, insofar as we are Americans at all, inhabitants of myth rather than history."

Manhattan was for me a mythical place, as magical as anything Dorothy would see on the Yellow Brick Road on the way to the Emerald City. Some landed by ship, like Donna and me, but many more traveled by land from towns throughout America to live in and love New York City. F. Scott Fitzgerald's Nick Carraway in *The Great Gatsby* describes the moment for many of us, when you cross a bridge into Manhattan, "with the sunlight through the girders making a constant flicker upon the mov-ing cars" to enter a city "where anything can happen."

It's a beautiful story, and many things have happened to many people in the city. But riding the subways to get to City College of New York as I had to do, gives you a different picture, less romantic, and more like work. But Manhattan remains a historical, mythmaking, place—once the home to thousands of talented artists, actors and writers leading ambitious, often threadbare, creative lives.

Sampling what we could, Donna and I embraced a myth or two, but we resisted other myths—ever restless, ever dissatisfied with our present circumstances, always looking for a tribal home.

"So, where *is* your home?" A friend confronts us.

"Wherever I can find Donna," I say.

Which brings me back to Seabrook. Aside from my instinct for trouble, what made me take her class? I wasn't one of her anointed. She wouldn't so much as place a pencil mark on my manuscript. Paul Theroux, a novelist and traveler of wide interests and indefatigable energy, offers good reasons for embracing challenging cultural journeys. He says, "The quest, the getting there, the difficulty of the road ..." is the most interesting part of any journey, but that aside, he adds that "the traveler's mood, especially—is the subject."

Everyone writing books is subject to a variety of moods. Moods that rarely matched my own, but every book had something to offer, per-haps obsession or surrender, maybe fantasy and mystery, entertainment wrapped in wit and criticism, sometimes even wisdom. Books breathe and smile, inform and mislead—they radiate energy.

Seabrook wrote a book I liked, which is why I signed up for her class. Then I discovered that Seabrook, the author, inhabited an Orwellian island with a sweeping totalitarian view I disliked.

The literary ecology remains a mystery to me. In theory, workshop participants are on the same team, enjoying the comfort of comradeship, wanting to help each other. Except this isn't true. The workshops are sporting arenas, a place for performance art. Few participants are completely open with each other. It's not unlike business strangers attempting a deal. Total exposure of one's intentions can lead to new demands, awkward challenges, perhaps even a sudden unraveling. So you hold your cards close to your chest to make sure no one sees them. No matter how much you reveal, the assumption is that there must be more that you're hiding. Which is likely to be true.

When Geoffrey Wolff writes on my manuscript "too private" he means I'm still the immigrant observer, uncertain of my welcome, an outsider inspecting the borders I'm facing—poking at the chain-link fence keeping me out, eyeing warily the natives, strangers to me.

In 1780 John Adams proposed: *I must study politics and war that my sons may have liberty to study mathematics and philosophy. My sons ought to study mathematics and philosophy, geography, natural history, naval architecture, navigation, commerce and agriculture, in order to give their children a right to study painting, poetry, music, architecture, statuary, tapestry, and porcelain.*

That's three generations. If Donna and I were to follow this generational pattern, she and I must suffer our hazardous businesses to win a break for our children by (1) having them—a huge decision (2) supporting them—as we should (3) hoping that unlike us, they wouldn't have to surrender their dreams.

The problem is: we don't want to surrender our dreams either. We've already cast ourselves adrift from conventional security by abandoning the professional employment Donna and I both enjoyed—and now we're attempting to make one more bargain with enterprise, one more deal in search of Fat City. We want to jump-start our own inner-third generation, which, as everyone knows, requires money.

I keep talking to Bollinger.

23

BEFORE BOLLINGER APPROACHED US WITH HIS HIGH-RISK, ALL-or-nothing gamble, Donna and I had survived several near-death experiences, one in an Alaskan avalanche, another in a private plane I was piloting, and a third in the sailboat I'd sailed into a hurricane. Some of us are attracted to risk, even self-destruction, but I never saw myself in that light. Attempting to keep our financial balance we're hoping that the printing store we've launched will offer us a smoother ride than my other piloting skills.

There isn't much talent required to buy or lease copy machines, rent a storefront and post signs announcing that you're open for business. But once you're in business there are many ever-changing challenges to staying afloat. As in writing, there's a hierarchy of effort and accomplishment. A wonderful short story is no less wonderful because it is short, but it is less than a wonderful novel of equal merit.

Donna decides to take on services outside the technical scope of a copy center, aiming to distinguish ourselves as a commercial printer, an expert source for high-resolution graphics and typesetting. This was before you could publish a book by using a laptop computer. Our competitors in this area are a handful, not nearly as many as there are copy and print stores.

We're experimenting with management. We don't use formal titles and believe in teamwork. The tension between believing and putting our beliefs into practice builds quickly. We've reorganized the staff, hired a new press operator, established job descriptions, a training checklist, altered the order-entry system, contracted for a new accounting system. "Hands-off consulting," might not be the best description of my limited effort working for Donna. What I haven't done is write enough to maintain my equilibrium as a writer.

The financial structure of a neighborhood shop is fragile, and training new people who join us is a large task. We didn't anticipate that we would be competing for some of the same talent that software companies wanted to hire. It wasn't unusual for mid-level software company execs to sidle up to one of our employees on the pretext of using our computer services to see if our employee could be tempted to join their software company.

Faced with such pressure, we hire the best talent that applies, and put up with a few eccentricities among our staff to keep our store open. A high IQ is always welcome, a high EQ (emotional quotient) too, though high EQ is more difficult to find.

It's Friday. The Bollinger negotiations are stalled, casting me into a dark mood blackened by the gray skies. I help a customer at the print store.

"I can get copies for less," he informs me. He's thin, proportioned to run a marathon. His bike helmet is marked by lightning bolts. I think of Mercury. A rich impasto of curls sprouts outside the cocoon of his helmet. The hair near his ears is wet from the sweat of biking. I wonder why he thinks it's okay to bring his bike into the store. Probably because it's custom built out of titanium and costs a fortune. I expect to see his ankles sprout wings; instead he retrieves a legal document from one of the panniers. I offer to copy and bind the materials he needs. The binding costs extra and could earn us a dollar more. But I'm no expert, or fast.

"I need it now," Mercury tells me.

Donna comes over. "No problem," she says. "Sorry for your inconvenience." But the man needs his ounce of flesh. His eyes sink deeper into Donna. "It's always like this," the man says. Other customers are listening, an embarrassed silence accepts the man's complaint, amplifies it. I wonder why he's in the store complaining. He must like something we do.

"We'll do it right," Donna promises, in a voice meant to sound cheerful.

Mercury receives his copies tucked inside a binder. He gives me another steely look. His helmet is still on. His thighs bulge with rider's muscle. He's wearing expensive Nikes that make his feet look extravagantly large. He tightens his chinstrap. His gloves are padded and there's room cut out for fingers. He leaves, I feel relieved.

"I'm all thumbs in this place," I say.

Donna, though outwardly calm, remains upset. Her surfaces have not been tempered to repel aggression. Sartre and others say that no one outside of ourselves can control our emotions—brave words, and difficult advice to put into practice.

One of our salesclerks, Bradley, has remained at a computer working undisturbed. The man is bright, tough, five foot six, a man with the quick movements that earlier communicated enthusiasm, but now shows impatience for work less stimulating than astrophysics, and he hates to be interrupted.

Bradley is a technical wizard. Donna is not into tech. She's willing to accept his abrupt manner as the price we must pay for expert knowledge. A bargain she's kept even after several customers walked out in a huff, offended by Bradley's what-a-pain-in-the-ass-to-help-you-ma'am manner. Donna is deciding slowly, very, very slowly, that she should fire the student, a process she affectionately calls "letting go," as if compelled to release precious illusions.

Our banker calls. "Who is that guy Bradley who wouldn't take a message for you?" We talk about a new loan, and hang up.

"You said you're going to get rid of Bradley?" I glance at Donna, but she isn't going to be outfoxed by me.

"Well," she says, "You know … It's *our* shop."

"You want me to do it?"

Donna is resigned, retreats. "No, I'll do it."

Bradley is at one of the company's computers. Donna goes over and has a chat with him. I'm in the back of the store standing guard. Donna returns perplexed, holding herself in the vague manner of someone caught unawares.

"What happened?" I ask.

"I don't know."

"You were supposed to fire him."

The store is empty except for a few employees. Donna cuts a check for Bradley's severance pay. I watch her approach him again. She pulls up a chair and hands him the check. She's talking through a tight smile, acting cheerful. I see him questioning her. She seems vaguely on the defensive. Is she admitting an error? The man has been a sweet toothache. The back of his neck is turning red. Donna is still smiling, a tense porcelain smile doggedly spinning an aura of pleasantness.

Bradley jumps up suddenly, check in hand. He flings his backpack over his shoulder and rushes for the door. Just outside he pivots and then runs back in. He isn't a large man, but taller than Donna. He raises his middle finger in a tribute favored by irate drivers all over North America, and shouts, "Fuck you, Donna." He runs out again.

Donna stands motionless and wide-eyed, by turns looking forlorn and confused. Is this a short story Bernard Malamud might have written?

"What did you say to him?" I ask.

"Well, I started by saying that we needed someone who could do better with customers." She takes a deep breath and exhales. "When I handed him the check I'm not sure if he thought that it was a bonus or something. He asked me if I'm firing him. I said that I don't like to use that word. He wanted to know if I was changing his hours. I said I just had to let him go. He asked me again if I was firing him and I answered again that I had to let him go. That's when he jumped up."

A business has many pleasures, but they aren't free. When you see a business advertised for sale "due to the owner's health," you can be sure it's not good health they're talking about.

The effort to run a company seems to be making us coarser. We're more alert to fraud and theft. In our former ventures, a pet store employee had to go for stealing; we also had to fire a salesman who sold rugs for cash and kept the cash. We're on guard, and on the defensive too much, acting as monitors rather than managers. We don't want to be defined by rude noises, coarse decisions, anger and disappointment. We would prefer a pastoral, our Arcadia, a prelapsarian Eden. We would like to be singing "Somewhere Over the Rainbow."

A literary agent offers advice: "Self-employment is one of America's favorite dreams, a book saying that it just ain't [always] so is not one which would find a place in the market. I'm sorry."

We're both sorry. Questioning received conventions is rarely welcomed.

Nonetheless we have sunk too much money and too much democratic effort to let the printing business collapse, to shrink like a sea anemone, regress into a dictatorship governed, as one novelist put it, by the owner's *hovering presence and sly attention*.

Donna hires an assistant sales and admin assistant to help her out—Cassandra, Cass for short. The start of our new hire is good. She's competent, friendly, engaging, tall and lanky, blonde, corn-blue eyes ever alert. She declares her loyalty to Donna, enjoys the work. Cass becomes the public face of our small shop. She likes to roam, to be here, to be there, and not be tied down to a desk guiding and encouraging other employees to make the venture prosper. That's the dull stuff. She reserves to herself the pleasures of friendship in a pleasant environment Donna has established. Several months into the job Cass's effort slips a little. Her partner drives her to work sometimes late, sometimes takes her away at odd hours. Donna's side pains return on account of all the pressure. Every modification, every move Cass now resists—purchase orders are an imposition on her first-name approach to doing business, morning meetings a pain.

A challenging service business can make anyone cranky. Donna and I are beginning to show plenty of the signs. We're watching for snake-bites, and feeling stones in our stomachs. We have four phone lines coming into the shop. Cass never has to leave the premises, but she has a pager. (This was before cell phones were as common as Kleenex.) I ask Cass, "Why the pager?" She says she must use her pager so her home-owners' association can reach her in case of an emergency. *Okay*, I'm thinking, and voice some possibilities: a tsunami could hit Seattle, a meteorite perhaps, the dreaded three-hundred-year earthquake we're all waiting for, your typical everyday Seattle emergency. Cass stares at me.

She has another excuse. She says the pager is a personal adornment. We're into legalities. I'm intruding on her privacy, her person. Can this be so difficult?

"Hell is other people," Sartre wrote.

I sense that Cass might be siphoning off business for her personal benefit. I forbid her to give out her pager number to our customers. A toothless threat, since I'm not at the store most of the time. I mention my concerns to Donna. She gives me her look, the disappointed look, the questioning look, the why-must-you-do-this-to-me look.

"She wouldn't cheat on us," Donna says.

"That's because you wouldn't cheat."

"You want me to cheat?"

I get the double meaning. She holds my hand for a moment to let me know that she doesn't mean it.

"We need a hard-nosed manager," I say. There's something impatient in my voice. My hope had been that Cass would have helped Donna in the hard-nosed department. I see an upwelling in Donna's eyes, a glance averted.

"I'm only me," Donna says.

I'm left defenseless, so I say defensively, "I don't want you to be anyone else."

We go to Ivar's Salmon House on Lake Union for dinner, and to talk. "Are we becoming collaborators in our own catastrophe?" I ask.

"Is that what you think?"

"I don't know what to think."

We're seeking mystery, adventure, the unknown in life. I find that in books, the outcast mind floating where it can, observing itself, fleeing a thought, jumping on a bandwagon, stretching time without losing consciousness. Donna finds it in nature, the flourishing gardens, the wild geese, the raptors and chipmunks.

We would like to think that we're egalitarian in every aspect of our life, but the work laboratory we had set up at the printing shop to discover new ways of interacting, new ways of conquering disorder and inefficiency, shows poor lab results. The company needs a touch of the Neanderthal, less proselytizing in the trenches and more return on investment. We haven't been able to reconcile our idealism with the reality of our experience. We've been unable to mark the border between vision and illusion.

"We need Caligula or Genghis Khan to rule this empire," I say.

"Try the salmon," she says.

"It's time to sell the business."

"The scalloped potatoes are good."

At the moment we're like two ships passing each other in the night. I've helped with the startup, but I claim to be a part-timer. She's not likely to listen to a consultant who happens to be her husband, but we make the attempt.

What distinguishes one retail service provider from another is often the consistency of the staff's smiles. We are losing our will to smile. The stress builds. Donna tears a ligament and comes to work with the help of a crutch. Cass accuses her of intimidating the staff to work harder by her example.

I'm learning how point of view works in fiction. Everyone has a point of view, which only rarely matches the points of view of other people witnessing the same action. But how much to say, and what to withhold?

Donna and I have our philosophical differences, too. I hold a bleak view. I believe that kindness expressed amid competitive commercial relationships may be misperceived as weakness, and a weakness in any competitive situation invites attack. I wish this wasn't so. I wish I could think otherwise. Her generosity is seen as a weakness by some of the staff, encouraging them to take self-serving attitudes. Twice I'm forced to return to the printing store for longer periods to keep the more aggressive employees in check. I move my writing to the margins of the day.

But if we must be shopkeepers, I would in fact rather own a printing store. My preference, though, would have been a store situated somewhere near Norman Rockwell's America, redolent with pepper-mint smells, kind voices, and smiling customers, but failing in that—I want to sell the business.

I bring it up to Donna more often.

Donna doesn't want to listen, or sell the business.

A coup seems to be brewing. A Cass-inspired whispering campaign has begun. The whispers get bolder. Donna's mood darkens; she's con-fused by the politics. Our wish to have an enlightened commercial republic crumbles despite all the effort. We have one foot in the practice of commerce, one foot in literature studies. We should visit Shakespeare more often to hear what Richard II or Henry IV has to say.

In a clash of cultures and goals we might be discussing Tennessee Williams and Emily Dickinson in the evening and negotiating our busi-ness survival in the morning. We're living two lives, one of great won-der found in the books that engage us and the other in a series of ven-tures to pay our bills. An effort that confounds us, slips sideways, seems to dissolve as we try to refocus. Other people seem to be leading normal lives: vacations, reunions, sabbaticals, weekend getaways. We're in the middle of the woods in midlife, and it's dark.

24

'M BACK IN BOLLINGER'S OFFICE, MORE EAGER TO TALK TO HIM. We've made some progress, and we've taken several steps back. It's unlikely that I'm only the second person he has approached. He's probably playing the field with several landowners and several investors. But he's not going to tell me that. He's been in the game for too long to reveal the entire hand dealt him. He can brag about the millionaire sports guys who are his customers, and he'll mention the entrepreneur artist Dale Chihuly who leased an expensive car that he wanted to repaint chartreuse. (Request denied.)

Bollinger doesn't lack for influential customers and wealthy friends. Why is no one jumping on his new dealership bandwagon? The knowledgeable investors must have reservations about investing. The smart money isn't betting on him. What's left is dumb money—Donna and me.

He's not interested in my background, but I'm interested in his, partly to gather material for the book, partly to understand the character of the man I'm facing. I mention, once again, the book I'm writing. He arranges an interview with his father.

His dad lives in Walla Walla—about forty miles east of Snake River where newly hatched salmon spill into the Columbia River in Washington State.

He's white-haired, unhurried. We're having lunch at a local eatery. He was careful not to invite me to his house when he agreed to the interview. A house, an apartment, can suggest many things about its inhabitant. It might reveal pride in possessions or expose careless indifference to housekeeping. You can see books or the lack of them. Maybe trophies, maybe too many cars in the garage, maybe nothing interesting. Possibly, too, he doesn't want to advertise living arrangements with another person not meant to be revealed to the public.

He removes the cellophane from a cigar. "A cheap cigar," he says, not lighting up. "I never could spend money." He takes a taste of his unlit cigar and then swallows a pill with a sip of water.

The Bollinger family comes out of central auto-dealership casting. In the early part of the last century Frank Bollinger, the grandfather, arrived with his teacher wife from Wisconsin to start a farming dynasty and failed. He then took to new technology: the automobile. "All you needed then was an oversized garage to win a dealership franchise," the father explains. There were once twenty-six franchised dealers competing to sell cars to a Walla Walla population of twenty-five thousand people.

Frank started selling the Marmon auto, then the Real, the Kole and the Dart car. And when these didn't survive he went on to sell the Star car, which led to the Durant, and when the Durant failed Frank formed a Chrysler dealership that his children inherited. (The typical way this is accomplished is by "selling" the business on favorable terms to one's son.)

As I listen, I'm coming to understand that nearly every Main Street seeker of fortune such as the Bollingers and me are looking to strike a moment in time and circumstances that rewards our meager skills. This pursuit may require courage; it always requires a commitment, invites rejection, demands persistence, but success remains iffy.

I'm back in Bollinger's Cadillac office the following week. I'm encouraged. The family has financial resources. I'm not sure how these assets are distributed within the family, and who controls what, but if I can get somebody with financial clout to guarantee Bollinger's lease I would have a strong insurance policy that would pay me if Bollinger's venture failed. We chatter about the weather, then segue into Lexus generalities, hopes, and possible rewards.

"Can we get your father to guarantee the lease?" I ask.

"Not a chance," he says.

I'm allowed to assume that his father served in the Pacific theater in WWII. To invest in a Japanese franchise would be tantamount to sleeping with the enemy. I don't know what to make of this. The way I would hear it later from Bollinger's sister, their father never came close to actual fighting, but was stationed in a noncombat zone where he tested aircraft tires for durability. It's possible I misheard one or the other sibling.

This much I know: Family members tend to hold on to profitable family companies with clenched fingers, either directly as manager-owners or via legacy trusts. They hold on to profitable opportunities, too. Why would they invite me to join this exclusive club? Donna and I have dipped our toes into several lakes of ignorance we should have been smart enough to avoid.

So I ask: "You want me to borrow gazillions to build a car palace for you that no one else will finance?"

My exaggeration doesn't earn me a smile. I'm left with the queasy impression, perhaps artfully misleading, that his father is skeptical about his son's aims and ambitions and potential for success, thus the need for an outsider like me to invest in a risky deal.

It occurs to me that John Wayne, riding his bronze stallion alongside us, wouldn't invest in a Japanese franchise either. It occurs to me that the Saab dealership the novelist Kurt Vonnegut owned and operated on Long Island nearly went broke. The skeptic in me rises quickly, riles easily. Bollinger's father won't invest. He won't guarantee the lease. I'm left to assume that memories of WWII linger. The surprise, the deceit, the images of arrogant warlords. The Bataan Death March, the Rape of Nanking. The Korean "comfort maids" enslaved to provide sex to Japanese soldiers. We're not talking about nice guys.

But new stories are taking the place of the old—stories of American auto dealers competing with each other to sell Japanese products, stories of consumers choosing overseas quality.

If I'm not Bollinger's first choice, he's not my first choice either. My first choice would have been to inherit a bucket of money to do with as I wish. But if I'm on the verge of making a bad decision, I'm in good company. The Washington State governor and several important-looking people are framed in autographed photos hung in his office to watch over us. He sees me looking at Mrs. Bush's autographed picture.

"That must have cost you a fortune in political donations," I say.

He answers offhandedly, almost negligently, "We gave them a car to use when they were here."

"So you're a Republican?"

I get a look of smiling indifference.

Our rules of engagement had followed the old pattern: Say as little as possible off-subject, avoid politics and religion, or anything remotely personal and stick to the optimistic. But the writer in me pushed on the walls closing us in. I believe commercial enterprise is personal, intimate, close-service, close-failure, close-combat—a game of good vs. bad, a game of survival. Despite such divergent views our conversation starts showing a peculiar grace and spark, pitched somewhere between friendly and conflicted.

He describes the formative years of his training. His mentor, a manager working for his dad, taught him how to appraise and sell a car, explaining, "Every car has its pluses and minuses. That year the ugliest part of the car was the bumper. 'You got to sell the ugly bumper first. Once you got the bumper sold, the rest is easy.'"

I draw a mental picture of a blossoming chrome piece formed into an anxious grimace. Since Bollinger didn't jump at the chance to buy the land, I have to assume he didn't have the money. His cash position is an ugly bumper, a handicap probably flagged in his franchise application. But if he can tell Lexus that he's nailed down a landlord, Donna and me, that weakness would be overcome, the ugly bumper made pretty. We're into another phase of our dealmaking. I'm not the dispassionate observer I would like to be. What I give up, he profits from. What he surrenders, I gain. I'm up to my ears in this thing.

But whenever I see him I'm left to wonder why neither of us want to admit that we won't reach the stellar achievements of the people we admire. Though I've once grown long hair to mourn the unarmed Kent students protesting the war in Vietnam killed by our National Guard, now it's closely styled, clipped. Though Bollinger was voted Mr. Rowdy by his high-school graduation class, how rowdy could anyone call the scrupulously polite Mr. Bollinger today? Where is the funk, the beat, the rhythm and music in our lives? Main Street has changed us. We've become practical to a fault.

I show him a revised *Car Palace* profile of our interaction. The sketch is headlined with a quote from Shakespeare to lend us encouragement: *"There is a tide in the affairs of men which, taken at the flood, leads on to fortune. Omitted, all voyage of their life is bound in shallows ..."*

Taken from *Julius Caesar*, a play that illuminates ambition, betrayal and envy, in the pursuit of power.

He likes the piece as much as the first one I showed him.

We have staked out our opposing claims against the unknown, prospecting for gold in our separate ways. We can only guess what other habits of triumph and competitiveness, what skill, what talent, what foresight, what discipline, timeliness, what large ambition, agility, management instinct, and good luck lead to anyone's outsized success.

Privileged by the accident of birth to be the son of a successful auto dealer who gets to buy into his dad's business, a nagging thought must pursue him—could he have made anything at all out of his life without dad's help?

The evidence is missing, or at least not definitive.

He's motivated to prove to his dad that he can do better. That aside, he can talk up a storm about this or that Cougar player or coach, and how they can improve their game. No doubt he has an opinion on how badly I'm playing my game. Yet he instinctively avoids troubling analysis.

This is what American-made optimism looks like, focused. The optimism that denies climate change, spurns health care for the needy, dreams of shutting down Medicaid, hates government, and has lost us young and vital American lives in the ill-conceived wars in Vietnam and Iraq. But it's also the optimism that has invited refugees such as me to try my hand at being an American. I'm grateful for the latter.

Politics aside, Bollinger and I take our cues from every public source that comes our way, and speak with the hushed air of conspirators. He hands me a glistening green tube containing Lexus architectural concept drawings to take to a local architect I know.

25

I VISIT A FRIEND WHO RUNS AN ARCHITECTURAL SERVICE OUT OF his home. Bearded and handsome in a pioneer sort of way, he is working on several projects, and freelancing at the Parks Department. A bachelor, he doesn't need much time for himself, an occasional weekend at his mountain cabin, or time with friends for a game of bridge. His porch creaks a little. I give the bell another push. He lets me in. I try to fend off his yappy dog, Kulshan. He orders Kulshan to keep quiet and provokes another paroxysm of barking happiness.

I explain my needs.

"I don't know, Ed," he says. Kulshan runs a leash around my feet.

"What don't you know?"

"I'm busy. I've got all this other work." His sweater is missing a few stitches. He must be thinking of buying another kayak.

"It's only a site plan," I say.

He looks at me, annoyed by my simplification. I add some spin, "You don't need to spend a lot of time. I'm looking for a sketch. It's speculative at this point." He manages to get Kulshan into a separate bedroom. The dog whimpers unhappily.

He works without help. His drafting table is in a space off the kitchen, facing greenhouse-slanted windows overlooking a ravine. The shipping cranes along the shore of Commencement Bay are visible. We've been sailing partners on many occasions. The Puget Sound averages just seven-knot winds year round, not enough to excite the larger displacement sailboat that replaced the smaller one Donna and I owned, but when it blows, it really blows. If small-craft warnings are up, and sailboats heeling out on the sound, he's the only man I know in my immediate circle who'll join me on short notice, leaving work and clients behind to rip across the Sound's crashing waves. For this I like him—he's no stuffy suit stuck to deadlines—but I'm also, at the moment, the business guy trying to get things done on time. His embrace of mutable deadlines worries me.

He glances at the green tube of architectural drawings I've brought. An element of frustration lies between us. I know he would rather go sailing, but I need a spec site plan next week. He says, "I'll have to look at the building codes, develop a traffic pattern. We need an idea of the elevations and a topog."

"Use the topography from the previous time," I urge. He had built the Abbey Carpet store Donna and I had operated. Since then we had attempted another building on the site, a theme restaurant that we abandoned before we broke ground.

He studies the drawings I brought. His enthusiasm languishes. He takes a pencil and holds it like an artist's brush. He sketches a few lines, some shadows. He's seeking out problems, difficulties, conundrums. He seems puzzled.

"What?" I ask.

"It's not that easy."

I plead my case. "I need to show something to the Lexus people. It doesn't have to be perfect." He agrees to do the site plan without being convinced that he should. I splash a wider circle around us. "There's Bollinger to satisfy. No one is going to be happy if we can't meet their national grand opening date." There are other complications too. "If this thing flies we'll need to have the drawings stamped." My friend meets my questioning look. Architectural design is how he earns his living, but he has never bothered to pass the requirements for state certification, so he can't certify his own drawings.

"It's not a big deal," he says. "I can get a structural engineer to check the drawings and stamp them when I need to."

A week later I return to look at what he's prepared. "What's this?" I ask.

"I thought I would do something different."

I study the plan, an elegant solution to a difficult site. "It's not the building they want."

He takes the drawings from me. "Look at how it uses the frontage. The common wall between the two buildings works out well."

"They're going to take one look at our plan and throw us out."

"It's better. Just look at the site."

"It's great work, but it's not the building they want."

We're not into much pretension. Lexus wants to look like a freestanding Lexus. They've given us a prepackaged design. Our job is to adapt the "look and feel" to the individual site and engineer it to meet local building code. He gives me a look he reserves for philistines, and agrees to do another take on the plan. I leave without saying goodbye to Kulshan.

26

ON MONDAY I'M ONCE AGAIN SITTING IN A VAST OFFICE reserved for Bollinger. You can fit four or five pool tables inside. Is he really comfortable working here? Alone? By sheer coincidence, I had done business with the previous owner of the Cadillac dealership that Bollinger had bought. The previous owner wanted his ho-hum office carpet to be replaced with an impractical but gorgeously plush white carpet to showcase an exquisitely detailed, small-scale, table-sized ceramic of Queen Elizabeth II's coronation carriage. He had a set of English teacups, too.

I prefer Bollinger's John Wayne to Queen Elizabeth II's coronation carriage. Joan Didion described Wayne as a man who could build a woman a house "at the bend in the river where the cottonwoods grow."

Bollinger takes a call from his daughter away at college. He wants to be a good father, think the right thoughts, do the right thing. I listen to his calm voice. He's a concerned father, a dutiful one. He hangs up and we get down to business. There's an interesting twist to our relation-ship. Now and then he must see me as a writer. An observer. Perhaps a critic. Maybe even a fan. And he plays his entrepreneurial role with a touch more swagger. I tell him that I could imagine him retiring as a Marine brigadier general, maybe even a major general. He nods his head in agreement, a forlorn look enters his eyes.

He's only an auto guy, one among thousands. In the privacy of his inner life, he must dislike the insistent demands of running a dealership, the repetition, each new season falling on the other, perhaps with changes in the size of taillights and sheet-metal work, or maybe a new model launch, but each new year is similar to the last—the same employee challenges, the same car manufacturers demanding million-dollar building upgrades, the same bankers bumping interest rates—even the advertising spin tends to get dull, nothing epic in the bundle of day-to-day worries percolating.

And he's not alone in those thoughts about the road not taken. Several forks in the road were ignored by Donna and me. Bollinger and I are now into sharing, filling in. It gives him license to go off-message. But only so much.

What has the boy voted Mr. Rowdy learned? Does the TV program *Dallas* capture his attention? What music rips through his heart? Does he watch MTV, listen to Michael Jackson? Why did the first woman he married, his high-school sweetheart, leave him?

The arena in which he and I compete is so utterly different from the fields others have conquered in their lifetimes. Tennessee Williams didn't have a financially helpful teach-me-the-ropes father. His father disliked him, cruelly mocked him. Bollinger's dad might have lobbed him into the pool when he was unable to swim, but he also made his son's career.

Ever agile, Bollinger seems to be wondering what makes me tick. He's an expert salesman, appealing, friendly, and always optimistic. He says he's late for the wheel-incentive meeting. I have no clue what such a meeting might entail. He explains that it's a "rouse the troops and reward the best of them" sales meeting. If you're a salesman, you can earn a bonus for selling specialty hubs and tires, for writing the greatest number of finance and insurance contracts, and, of course, for selling the most cars.

Bollinger has advanced his company's fortunes with persistence. Sometimes he's not up to a morning sales meeting and his opening joke might not sound as good as when he practiced it. He conducts weekly sales meetings, monthly awards events. No smoke and armor here, no lock and load, no clanging vehicles or stunning swordplay. We're not talking about a cavalry charge either. Much of the work grows tedious from repetition but remains necessary. As soon as you stop repeating these mundane tasks, the sales carousel stops.

He invites me to attend a meeting organized by the Toyota Lexus division in Torrance, California. I jump at the chance. I tell him I'd like to interview one of the Lexus division executives for the book I'm writing. Sure, he says, he'll help if he can.

We're competing to be nice to each other. But each of us pays our own way to get to Torrance. My request for an interview is slipped through a series of official Lexus hands, each enthusiastic, affirmative, and inconclusive. I'm living in the land of no "no's." Every phone conversation seems to add promise. Success around the corner. For a time this is a very pleasant sensation, lulling. I don't expect any difficulty. I call one of the interview prospects directly. His secretary answers and forgets to put my call on hold. She's talking to a man, who isn't pleased.

"This should be handled by publicity," he snaps.

He won't even say hello to me on the phone. She hangs up. I call publicity. Publicity promises to get back to me. "When?" I ask. Maybe in an hour, maybe later. Maybe much later. I log four more calls. Each time the voices I hear are positive, assured, "no problem" voices, but no one can pin down a time, or a person to interview. I'm getting desperate. I call again. I wait.

One of the Toyota people sounds a sympathetic note. He tells me that the job of the Americans in publicity is to protect the Japanese from the media. "We can't have them saying what they think."

Prime Minister Nakasone had suggested that America's troubles with education can be traced to an impure gene pool. This was a clunker in contemporary American ears. The Japanese caused another public relations brawl when local press revealed they would build a private Japanese school in Palos Verdes that excluded girls from the school.

"Our Japanese executives are now very reluctant to talk to the media," my source explains. He tells me that the lines of authority are murky when it comes to Japanese executives. "They're a small number here. They come and go, attend any meeting they want." After a hesitation, he adds, "We listen to them."

At the nearby motel where I'm staying I can get a Japanese newspaper, along with the complimentary local paper, *The Wall Street Journal* and *USA Today*. A white limousine arrives to take Bollinger and me and several dealers to inspect mock-up dealership interiors. A Toyota dealer riding with us chortles with pleasure about his future. "Sure, I listen to them [Toyota]. They kiss my ass and I kiss theirs. We make nothing but money."

After the tour, we attend a convention-like Lexus gathering. I remember the men; it was mostly men, a testosterone-loaded male gathering eager to catch the next new thing. The smell of new cars, the pliant feel of leather, and the air of ambition combine in a volatile mix.

In the Northwest, Bollinger is known among local auto dealers, but in this overheated male society he is a small-town boy trying to make it big among the megadealers attending. He's more outgoing, laughs

more, shows a full set of happy teeth, eyes shining, eagerness showing. He's generous, introducing me in his usual outgoing manner. Many
faces, lots of chatter. Boys with toys. The money, the energy, the vibrant
talk—hopes are riding high.

Bollinger approaches a man whose prosperity seems to cling to him
with the glint of gold bullion. I tag along. The imperialism of money,
of privilege, has a colonizing effect on those near. Bollinger, too, glows
brighter. But there's also a touch of anxiety pushing to overcome some
inexplicable uneasiness. He's greeting the dynamo dealer, an auto-industry lion, and must feel like a kid at a Big Daddy gathering. He hesitates,
looks at me, and there's another pause, a slight but embarrassing pause.
I'm the guy without whom he can't join the Lexus club. He waves in my
direction, casual, even dismissive, an afterthought. "Here's my contractor," he says.

My sudden demotion as Bollinger's hired hand startles me. A
moment ago we were an energetic twosome, respectful of each other,
a risk-taking duo. I suppress a quick retort and leave the two men to
talk business.

What else do I remember about southern California? The Los Angeles
County Museum of Art comes to mind, the Norton Simon Museum,
the Pasadena Rose Bowl, where our son will join the Husky team, and,
of course, Disneyland, where Donna and I had taken the children when
they were young. On the writer's side, there are F. Scott Fitzgerald and
Nathanael West and William Faulkner putting in their unhappy time as
Hollywood scriptwriters, Raymond Chandler famously inventing Philip
Marlowe, and Dashiell Hammett creating Sam Spade.

I return to Seattle and find a letter from my literary agent reporting
that she'd sent my book proposal to another publisher. At the printing
store the same issues keep percolating.

"The chaos is only temporary," Donna assures me. "Everything will fit."

"I'd like to escape from all this."

"Escape to where?"

"Anywhere. Together, though."

27

THE PICTURES ON THE WALL OF BOLLINGER'S OFFICE SHOW the ever-affable auto dealer with a perma-grin. Some pictures show him with women in billowy gowns standing alongside new cars, some show him and automotive executives exchanging plaques, awards. One picture stands out. Bollinger is on his knees on a gymnasium floor, dressed in a wrestler's uniform. He's wrestling a muzzled bear in a masculine spectacle staged for charity. He says that he hated the smell of the bear's breath.

The cultural transformations brought on by feminism are absent here. The suggestion that the best minds might be androgynous, collaborative, man-womanly, or woman-manly, wouldn't lighten this office. My father carrying his PhD gracefully suggests a diplomat's self-restraint. Bollinger's father fielding a football suggests physical prowess and domination. I don't think I would have wrestled a bear as Bollinger did. But who knows? The opportunity never came up, except for the time in Alaska when a grizzly ran past Donna and me and crashed into the woods. We stayed in the car until the bear sounds receded.

Bollinger is gesturing with a football referee's timeout signal. Our goalposts are far apart and we have come to another negotiating impasse. I'm not much into spectator sports, and hypermasculinity escapes me, but I expect more hand-to-hand combat. The excellent Steve Almond, an outspoken advocate of self-publishing, the author of *Against Football: One Fan's Reluctant Manifesto*, has suggested that "A big part of being a sports fan is dealing with male anxiety by forming a defensive huddle of dudes."

Maybe it's true. I wouldn't know. If Donna and I hadn't always been together, possibly I could have been one of the anxious guys Almond describes huddling with dudes, but for me, women, their many-patterned engagements with life—dealing with men and friendships and family, sports if they choose, beauty when it pleases them, work and careers, and giving birth—interested me more than chest-thumping, ass-patting bro talk.

The only "sport" that I took up in college was the rifle range, which wasn't a sport; it was target shooting, an opportunity to practice controlled breathing and steady trigger pressure. I did like lacrosse, a contact sport with a small ball at play, and I would have joined the team had I not also been working two jobs in addition to going to college.

In sharp contrast, Bollinger merely followed his father's male-centric Cougar-fan footsteps. He's not the most reflective man I've met, but he must question some of his decisions. The Marines made an officer out of him. He loved the service, and his job as executive officer of a Mediterranean landing team, and wanted to stay in the service. His father had other plans: "You can stay in the Marines if you want. If you do your auto career is over. I'm selling the business." The younger Bollinger caved without a fight, and returned to Walla Walla. His father's general manager mentored him and then, "Dad made me sales manager, and afterward general sales manager."

Bollinger's mother was at his side, backing him up, encouraging him. Her confidence in him gave him much confidence. By the time I meet him he's become an optimist in ways that I'm not. He expects to win each bet as if the dice are loaded in his favor. The dice in my hand don't feel as hot. I'm also writing a novel in which the main character is untrustworthy. This doesn't prepare me to be trusting.

Bollinger shrugs again. I ask him what accounts for his optimism.

"I didn't have any worries," he says, "a normal good childhood. Dad provided for my education. I had security, a loving mother, the strongest figure in my life. My mother worked at the dealership, my aunt was the bookkeeper."

According to Bollinger's sister, their mother, known as "Dynamite" to some, did every administrative thing at the dealership to help it grow from a faltering enterprise into a profitable one.

With more money, marital trouble came too. It's not clear if Bollinger's father had already taken up with a younger woman. But without warning, and with unspeakable callousness, he asks his son to fire his own mother, the hard-working, devoted, ever-loyal wife, described by the son as "the strongest figure in my life."

"Dad shouldn't have asked me to do that … It was a terrible thing, horrible."

Bollinger isn't a man to suffer regrets, but this memory registers the shock of remorse.

"What happened?" I ask.

Bollinger is unable to speak for a moment. His face is strained. He squirms a bit, catches his breath.

He fired his mother.

Pop culture might have influenced his decision to knuckle under dad's fist. "It's not personal, Sonny. It's strictly business," says Michael Corleone in *The Godfather*.

But this was different. This was mom.

In the tradition of unexamined gender models, he's also a man's man, like his father. His sister gave me an example of how this worked: Bollinger was afraid of deep water and didn't know how to swim, but his father was determined to force him to learn. The training consisted of tossing Bollinger into the pool unaided. He would struggle and gasp and come to near drowning before his father would haul him out.

My engagement with male cultural expectations had its own ups and downs. There was the *Mechanix Illustrated* magazine's heavy-lifting, bicep-busting Charles Atlas ads that tempted slim boys like me to become muscular demons of irresistibly dominant flesh. But failing in that pursuit, I learned to fly an airplane—up and down the Chugach Mountain Range in Alaska; and to recover from my small sailboat disaster, I subsequently mastered an ocean-going sloop. Small accomplishments, true. We take what we can reach.

We get back to business. Bollinger starts talking to the floor, not a good sign. "I read your letter. Mike has read it, so has my CPA." He falls silent and we wait a moment. He starts anew, "Mike thinks you're sincere." Bollinger's voice sounds provisional, ready to revise his general manager's opinion.

Another sticky wicket. Another *i* to dot, another *t* to cross. We've been here before. We've traveled the same route. Our dealmaking is not like a slalom that goes from top to bottom. The repetitiveness can get on one's nerves. Are we wasting our time?

I've gotten preliminary estimates on the cost of the building that he and Lexus want us to build: hundreds and hundreds of thousands of dollars above Bollinger's low-ball estimate. I'm not sure if that means that Bollinger has been as uninformed as starkly as I've been ignorant, or that he suspected all along that the price would come in high and blow the deal before we got it going.

He's wealthy, but he's not wealthy enough to avoid bankruptcy if his dealership fails and he needs to bail out of the lease—which he can easily void in a reorganization bankruptcy. Donna and I would be left holding the proverbial bag, empty. He's proposing marriage. A commercial one. Can we walk down this aisle? Can we trust this man? How long will the marriage last? He gives me a sidelong glance, perhaps to check his bearings before speaking again.

We've met with lawyers, his and mine, but we haven't signed final papers. I'm telling him that I can't do the deal. Why would Donna and I want to borrow huge amounts of money by mortgaging everything we own if at the end of the lease we would have a vacant special-purpose building and still owe a huge amount of money to the bank with no way to pay?

Bollinger uses his listen-to-this-I-can't-believe-it-myself voice. He jumps to a military metaphor and claims that my tent is falling down on my knees. He wants me to know that he wouldn't sue me for bad faith, and he wants me to know that he could. But we have no contract.

I've been consistent in reminding him that despite his vow that we have "an agreement to agree" we have no oral contract either, no moral requirement to continue. Only a signed final lease will get us out of the door to see the Emerald City.

We are in a corner of sorts. A corner we've made for ourselves. The thing about a large, even a threatening decision, is that no one wants to make a final commitment until the eleventh hour. We've been talking, just talking. But now that he says he has the franchise and I've learned I can't afford to build the more expensive building within the financial framework we'd discussed, we're once again knocking heads.

For a year and a half, he and I have teetered between openness and evasion, between cooperation and competition, each of us retaining our secrets and at other times overwhelming each other with candor. The conflict between writing and business, revelation and goal, truth and packaging, strikes every page, remains unresolved. I can't imagine that John Wayne riding his bronco alongside us, a man of few words, could vacillate so much. But who knows—how many wives did he have? Unlike Norman Mailer he didn't stab any of them. Bollinger will clock in at only three wives, same as John Wayne. I have Donna. Donna has me.

28

AT PASCO, NO MORE THAN AN HOUR AWAY ON A LEISURELY drive north from Walla Walla where Bollinger grew up, I see where he would have taken in the wide rolling hills, the deep green orchards and irrigated lands sloping skyward. What isn't irrigated is beautiful, too—sagebrush and prairie grass, especially in the spring when muted greens form a silvery fuzz on the hills, which the sun burns orange in the evening.

Walla Walla County is farm country rich in fertile soil, water, and good weather, a place of wheat fields, grape vines, hops, a cornucopia for vegetables. After WWII agriculture ascended a twenty-year wave of prosperity riding stable commodity prices, growing markets, and a supportive government agricultural policy. This was a time when the price of farm acreage blossomed in value, each new acre priced higher than the last, and the number of land millionaires multiplied along with the size of the crops.

To its locals Walla Walla became "a fine place to raise a family," a place where pundits pondered in print, "Why Walla Walla?" to describe its charms.

Donna is driving. We're taking a break from work. "If we get Bollinger wrong, we'll go broke," I say. "How do you read him?"

"How can you expect me to answer that? I haven't met him."

The tension wears on us. Any business has its ups, unanticipated downs, and dead ends. The auto business is notoriously cyclical, and we're not even in it yet.

Our printing store hasn't failed, nor has it made a breakthrough. We're in the oceanic muddle of all middles, the middle passage. We keep hoping the printing business will grow larger to provide the revenue to hire and keep the skilled workers we need to serve a demanding public.

The owners of small businesses are leagues away from the world of capitalist investors. Most small business owners have only their labor to invest. But this is not how the employees of a shop see you. Our payroll expense is larger than that of most stores our size. Cass believes that's Donna's problem. It doesn't stop Cass from asking for more help. Donna wants me to explain the slim numbers to Cass. I don't expect the conversation to go well.

During my next meeting with Bollinger we return to trading jokes. I'm once again half-consumed by the cushy office couch.

"Maybe a hamburger place would want to lease the building after I leave?" he says. I smile. To cover his auto-dealership mortgage I would need a half-dozen hamburger restaurants stacked on top of each other.

The layers of dealmaking can be many or few, transparent or opaque. Each is a barrier whether seen or not. A week earlier I had no idea what additional rent I might reasonably seek if I were to go ahead with the deal. I asked Bollinger's real-estate agent for advice; I asked a lawyer; I called three other brokers. I weighed the answers and reached for the highest number I could mumble without embarrassment. The amount of rent that an auto dealership can pay astonishes me, even if most of it would go to repaying the mortgage.

Nonetheless, Bollinger doesn't like the rent I'm quoting. We're at a dead end again, replaying an ancient market ritual by turning our backs toward each other. I'm convinced I can't budge; he's convinced he can't budge. Yet I'm probably the most willing fool he's found after hitting up a dozen potential investors. He must see, as I do, the rapidly spreading cracks in our business friendship.

My writing persona and my business persona are teetering toward a personality disorder. I must trust him to know what he's doing. He needs to trust Toyota and Lexus. Both of us must believe that this car requested by no one will thrive in a crowded market.

At home, Donna and I weigh the possibilities. It appears that we've miscast ourselves as business actors. She will not solicit new business at the printing store. We've fled some of our old-world traditions, but we're not embracing enough of the new. "I'm not good at selling," she says, which is why we had hired Cass.

What's to explain our serial entrepreneurship? Well, for one thing, we'd failed to find gold in the entrepreneurial gold rush so far. Though we're not doing anything unique at the print store, perhaps we can change, flutter near the edges of inspiration, alter the world a copy at a time? But with a thousand copy shops nearby we're not doing much. Maybe soon, maybe later?

29

I ASK MIKE LANE, BOLLINGER'S GENERAL MANAGER, OUT TO LUNCH.
He's fond of good food. He likes his suits well crafted. The restaurant
he suggests is removed from the pageant of signs guarding Highway
99. I discover a warm seafood salad—scallops, shrimp, and cod—which
sounds healthy except for the reason I like the salad, what makes it
warm, what wilts the lettuce: bacon and hot bacon drippings. Lane
orders grilled salmon.

The one-, two-, or three-martini lunch of *Mad Men* is not what we
do on Main Street. It's water and coffee for us. We're telling stories to
each other, bonding, making sense of the distance traveled. The more
competitive the livelihood, the more outrageous the stories told. Mike
offers a car story. He says that early in his career he had quit his job at an
auto-body shop, a place of dust and fumes, mouth and nose guards, to
take a job as a used-car salesman.

In those earlier days your small dealership could be a one-story building that had a porch in front of the showroom. On sunny days the salesmen could slouch and watch nervous buyers drive onto the dealership lot.

Lane describes his first day. He needs to use the bathroom. A fellow salesman tells him to take the elevator. (That's the joke—it's a one-story building.) A novice has so many things to learn. Unless you're the dealer's favored son soon to inherit the business, the education can be jumpy.

Lane stands on the porch, bold and ready, young and eager, trying to work himself into the good graces of the experienced salesmen. Lane says, "A customer drives onto the lot. Even from a distance I can see the carotids on the guy's neck. His face is red. He skids to a stop and jumps out. I'm thinking the guy is going to have a coronary.

"A few of the salespeople retreat indoors. I think this man is going to kill us. But the salesman who sold him the car doesn't move. He greets the customer who is sputtering unintelligibly and waving his bank payment book. 'You said,' the customer yells, nearly out of breath. 'I'm gonna have twenty-four payments to make. This here book says thirty-six!'

"'Lemme *see* that!' The salesman grabs the guy's payment book and flips through it. 'They did it again!' He shakes his head. 'Those banks, they keep on making the same mistake, over and over.' The salesman tears out the last twelve payments from the payment book, shreds them into little pieces and hands the book back to the customer. 'That'll take care of you.' The salesman smiles and the customer, feeling foolish now, smiles, and drives away happy."

Lane explains that salespeople would sometimes write in the *amount* of the payment but leave the *number* of payments blank, "for the girl in the office" to finish the paperwork. The salesman disappeared the next week, taking the girl in the office with him."

Lane laughs. I laugh, too. The story sounds ridiculous, and it's meant to be amusing. The truly rogue, if he and I ever had it, left us long ago. Around the time Lane started his sales career my brother held a sales job at a used-car dealership in Minneapolis. He said that noisy car differentials and transmissions were sometimes quieted with a judicious application of sawdust. When I mention this to Bollinger, he says, "I hate those old-time hustlers. They've ruined it for us." His Cadillac dealership has a high customer-satisfaction score. It's what gets you attention in car circles these days.

That aside, an antiregulatory streak appears to be imbedded in portions of the auto industry. Though carbon emission control is the defining imperative of automotive design and engineering, in 1974 Chrysler recalled 800,000 cars after it was caught installing a secret device in car radiators to defeat pollution controls and increase mileage. Hidden in the car's radiator? Who would have thought of that?

In 1995 Cadillac paid a $45 million fine and recalled half a million cars equipped with computer software to shut off the emission controls whenever the air-conditioner was turned on. In 2015 Volkswagen's software engineers designed cheater "defeat devices" to dupe emissions tests into believing that the cars were in environmental compliance while spewing out giga amounts of carbon exhaust.

The New York Times also reports that General Motors Vice Chairman and afterward Chrysler president, Robert A. Lutz, dismissed emission rules as "trying to cure obesity by requiring clothing manufacturers to make smaller sizes." He's not alone among government critics. Henry Ford II, railing against airbags, called them "a lot of baloney."

Fortunately for us in the USA, federally mandated new technologies like airbags, antilock brakes, electronic stability controls have reduced highway deaths nearly five-fold for every one hundred million miles travelled—saving a stunning number of lives every year, forcing even Robert A. Lutz to admit, "There was definitely a role for government in automotive safety."

What am I to make of this information?

The angle of light, the measure of candor is often limited to one's point of view. But deception is not what I think of when I think of working with Bollinger. His formative experience was in a small town where honesty is enforced by the absence of anonymity, and community memories linger a long time.

30

I'S EARLY SPRING, A BEAUTIFUL DAY, ONE OF THE YEAR'S BEST with crisp sunshine and casual breezes. The river and inlet waters fed by Puget Sound tides are sparkling as if sprinkled with melting cracked ice. Donna and I are trying to put off the need to make a final, irrevocable decision.

As we make our way into the La Conner countryside again the tension grudgingly dissipates. Each spring a million flowering bulbs bloom, dividing the fertile fields into colored stained-glass windows that appear to have fallen from the sky.

With such beauty before us, money and management chores fade from our attention. But the backdrop remains, a canvas of enterprise and money. Our printing company doesn't have depth of management. It's a rare small enterprise that does. The trivial and the large all land on the owner's desk. There's no cushion of money to protect us if we fall. No money to hire staff more experienced than ourselves. And there's the additional worry that at a moment's notice a key employee will abandon us. A small business is so personal: the betrayals and thefts feel damaging beyond their actual monetary value. It makes you wary, cautious. The lessons are intimate rather than academic. It's easy to implode from all the pressure.

Street smarts are needed to learn the ropes in a business. The beguiling nature of money held in people's hands often changes them. If you grew up lacking money, as most people do, this often prepares you for the hurly-burly hustle of making money. But not in every case. My father, growing up poor, remained principled, upright, a diplomat, professor and economist, a trustworthy man and a pious one. Street smarts weren't imbedded in my father's scholarly work. He didn't feel comfortable with money's motility, how it trickled down or siphoned up. Money was an intellectual idea that he grappled with as if it were a floating substance, fungible, an emollient that oiled economic demand and supply curves.

People didn't seem to enter into it, not enough anyway.

He couldn't visualize the flesh and the flash that showed men and women at oblique angles in the pursuit of money, in turmoil, in doubt, what a novelist would call a "scene," what an editor might call "action on a narrative arc," perhaps a page-turner, engaging, informative, maybe even suspenseful.

This revelation that my erudite father didn't understand how money flowed in the gutters as well as the moats surrounding academic castles startled me in the way that children who admire their parents are always startled by unwelcome revelations. The theories that he understood and taught to his students at Seton Hall University never quite fit the squiggly slant of commercial minds that he met in Manhattan who were selling limited real-estate partnerships. As it turned out, all of his investments were without value at the time of his death, though the stock certificates were handsomely printed.

A lack of money was the reason he partnered with another man to purchase our house in Brooklyn, a three-story brownstone with the top floor rented. It sold for $8,000 back in the early '50s. Our house-sharer and part-owner was a physician and a gardener. He cultivated our back-yard as a pastoral bulwark against the past that included his imprison-ment in a Nazi concentration camp. Roses were his specialty. The influx of Japanese beetles devouring leaves was a steady summertime aggra-vation. A survivor of the Nazi's Stutthof concentration camp (110,000 prisoners with 85,000 dead victims,) he was recognized as Righteous Among the Nations by Israel for helping Jews during the Holocaust.

Behind our brownstone stood an apartment building, a wall of urban living, reminiscent of the Ashcan School of painting and photography. There were clotheslines haphazardly strung from window to window, and in our backyard, too, we stretched a clothesline. On hot summer nights dozens of fireflies leaped out of the darkness to flash a reddish orange green. On those warm rose-scented nights, my father would sit in the backyard smoking a cigar or his pipe, alert to the occasional air-borne garbage bag tossed from one of the tenement building windows. He never yelled at anyone, and his criticisms were thoughtful, carefully voiced, both traits that made him an excellent diplomat.

A huge maple grew in front of our brownstone. Old World echoes must have moved my father and mother to buy this house on Kosciusko Street, a street named after an American Revolutionary War patriot from Poland.

TV in our time was a novelty. We had one. A large disk in front mag-nified the ten-inch screen. Air conditioners were expensive, bulky, and a luxury that we couldn't afford. It helped that we lived a half-block from St. Ambrose Church. My father went to pray and meditate and hear Mass nearly every morning. Conveniently, the parish supported a paro-chial school I attended.

I admired my father. He was an émigré leader seeking to free Lithuania from Russian occupation. The Russians, then called Soviets, and the

Russians who predated the Soviets, called czarists, and the Russians of today under the neo-Nazi Putin (described by one American president as having a "good heart") all have the same game plan: Trample the little guys, seize their land, enslave them. America has been staunch in speaking out against such colonization, for which Lithuanian Americans remain grateful.

I went to Webster Hall on Eleventh Street in the East Village to hear my father speak a number of times. The main event was politics, but the chief event for the youth attending was the dance that followed the speeches. We were not the rebellious youth of Patti Smith's East Village looking to break loose, not the kids who would later learn never to trust anyone over thirty. We were traditional, and conservative, without knowing it.

I first met Donna at a Lithuanian winter camp for youth, and after that we sometimes met at Webster Hall. She was as thin as a sparrow and lush with dark eyes and dark hair. The dances—the tango, the Lindy, and the fox trot, not to mention the waltz—kept us busy. The one, *two*, three beat of the waltz and the two quick-quicks followed by the slow step in the five-step tango ran a confused rhythmic competition in my head.

Some parents danced, but most of them sat on the wooden folding chairs that were moved to the sides to clear space for a dance floor. It was a perfect place to monitor youth. We learned how to dance without the attendant hope or opportunity for a follow-up lesson in quick seduction.

Though my father was celebrated and distinguished and pursued a stellar cause, at home, which served as his office, he was too busy grading papers, writing for several publications, and preparing political lectures to have much time, or interest, in anything not directly involved with his work. In our home there was no unwieldy confusion between public and private lives; the public life dominated.

I liked the doctor sharing our house, Dr. Starkus. My father liked the doctor, too. The pictures prior to my father's death show my mother vacationing with the two men near Atlantic City. The doctor, though a Nazi-camp survivor, was the bon vivant in our household. Gregarious and cheerful, he drank too much, and so did my mother. Since my father was ever diplomatic, careful, thoughtful, always self-controlled, he drank little, and tended to become sleepy if he did.

The excursions the three of them took to visit East Coast beaches they captured in photos. It looked like fun. At home, the kitchen table often turned into a robust friendly gathering with the two men's laughter competing—my father's laugh restrained, the doctor's voice loud, even boisterous, in full-blown appreciation of my mother's cooking skills.

When I learned that the doctor was also my mother's lover (a subject for another book), I was torn between the two men. I didn't know how to remain loyal to everyone at once. It must have been around that time I decided I wanted to become more like Tom Sawyer and Huck Finn. Since I was reared with the hysterical views of the Catholic Church that denied every aspect of human sexuality not locked down in the service of reproduction, it was a good thing that sex didn't enter into Tom's and Huck's stories.

Looking back on those days, I think my father, who admired the doctor's courage but not his poaching on my mother's affections, suffered in a deep silence that shortened his life. I've wondered since why my parents didn't divorce. They owned reams of social and intellectual capital, but little of the spendy kind. Money and education separated poor Catholics from rich Catholics then as they do today. Rich Catholics could have a marriage annulled, or live apart; poor ones went to confession. We weren't poor, but far from rich.

What I remember today of my parochial schooling is mainly this: I was in the seventh or eight grade when Sister called me out of the class to perform the duties of a godfather at the church baptismal. Apparently there was a no-show, a godfather on the lam, and they needed someone to get on with the ritual. Why not a dutiful kid? Sister didn't ask my parents for permission to employ my shallow godparenting skills. My mother probably would have laughed. My father would have argued that I was unprepared for those duties. Nevertheless, I stood at the baptismal as the godfather for a child while the priest performed the baptism. I hope today that my godson, an African American, has reached remarkable achievement in life. In my fantasy world I'd like to imagine he was Henry Louis Gates Jr.

I never mentioned my godfather role to my parents. At my age, I knew I couldn't live up to the task. Why was I chosen to be a godfather? Possibly because I grew up in an era of right-wing, obsessive, patriarchal Catholicism subservient to authoritarian popes. I believed in a Virgin Mary untroubled by sex, and her Assumption into heaven. My Catholic education left me startlingly ignorant about sex. Pope Francis will one day speak of the "erotic dimension of love" and the "stirring of desire" and conclude that such "is a marvelous gift from God." But an adolescent in my time tied to the panic-stricken chaste Church sex teachings, and pummeled by desire, was damned to daily sin.

To guard me from the crushing hormonal onslaught doing God's and nature's powerful work, I posted a three-inch-high plastic statue of the Virgin Mary on my elementary school desk. The Virgin wore blue and white and had her hands folded in prayer. This must have impressed the nuns and influenced them to choose me as godfather. There were several crevices and cracks in my faith, and my suspicion of pious authority increased steadily in my adolescent years and then rocketed into orbit during my early teens when a foolish and beautiful nun dramatized how people were tortured in hell to make them regret their sins. I suspect today that she must have studied the medieval horrors painted by Hieronymus Bosch, or perhaps she fell into sin because she was more beautiful than her mother, and her mother hated her for it.

Though there's much of the metaphysical and metaphorical in Catholic teachings that can be imaginatively reinterpreted to soothe contemporary morality, children tend to take things literally, and so did I. I didn't want to believe that *my* God willfully kept sinners alive in hell for eternity merely to torture them. In my child's mind this seemed unfair. (In my adult mind, too.) From *King Lear*, "As flies to wanton boys, are we to th' gods, / They kill us for their sport."

Without understanding theodicy, I fled from the god of terrible retribution, a jealous and vengeful god, neither omniscient, omnipotent nor all-loving as I was taught, a god unable or unwilling to help innocent and good people suffering without reason or justice.

My escape from Catholic dogma became an essential part of my moral and intellectual education. That aside, some years later my mother asked Donna and me to baptize our children, who were then toddlers. I inquired with the local Catholic priestly authorities how best to arrange for our children's sacrament of baptism, which according to Catholic beliefs could ensure their eternal salvation.

A dimwitted priest who went on to became an obstinate bishop declined to baptize the children on the basis that I wasn't a parishioner contributing financial support to his parish. I argued that money aside, which I was willing to pay for the service, the baptisms were intended to save the children's souls and not my own, which I was capable of handling without his sacerdotal help.

The baptism of our children was denied.

But mothers, my mother especially, are not so easily put off. She insisted that the children be baptized and she wanted to be present. I paid for my cousin, a Roman Catholic Jesuit priest, to fly from Chicago to Seattle to baptize the kids. Which he did at our house. Mom was present, pleased to have saved our children. The children, now adults, are satisfied too.

31

THE PRINTING STORE IS AT A WATERSHED, BUBBLING SOFTLY
along, lingering in the space between owner's pride and financial marginality. It's a fiercely competitive business, hectic with
small jobs, quick turnaround, erratic workloads, and many details to get
right. It's on the edge, we say, soon to become resoundingly profitable
were it not for our quirkiness as managers. Though we like the printing business, and enjoy the ebb and flow of people in a busy place, our
progress seems Byzantine compared to Bollinger's uncomplicated dad-
to-son dealership journey. The idea of selling the store starts recurring.
My voice subdued, intentionally low as if afraid to be heard, I mention
again that I would like to take up Don Quixote's lance to try my luck
with windmills, writing. If the car palace venture takes off I promise
Donna that we'll be done with business.

The real-estate agent calls me again. "Ed, would you mind signing
a promissory note regarding my commission?" I hear an uncomfortable cough. The sale he had anticipated between Bollinger and me
fell apart. He's done nothing useful since the introduction. We could

argue that a commission may not be owed at all on a build-to-suit. If you're a titan or a mogul, that's called playing hardball. But I'm not a titan or a mogul, nor expect to become one. Nevertheless, long-term legal commitments always give me pause. Promissory notes stop me dead in my tracks. "Look, I don't have a problem paying your commission once I get the money from Bollinger to pay it. I can't sign anything until I know where I stand. If the guy doesn't sign a lease I can live with, you're out of luck."

The agent persists. "My company thinks I should have something in writing." I tell him that if the deal goes through he'll get paid the same amount as if Bollinger had bought the land.

After advancing to this stage of shaky optimism, I'm curiously detached. I still don't think that our chances are solid. I'm short on positive mental attitude. I think about destruction, total ruin. Which might explain why I'm not ruined. I need to engineer a MAD pact with Bollinger: mutually assured destruction. No clever escape clauses in the lease. If Donna and I are going to bet all of our assets on Bollinger's success, we want him to bet all of his. If we have to go bankrupt because he fails or refuses to pay his rent, we want to make sure that he and his wife go bankrupt, too. The Mexican standoff. Pistols aimed both ways. I need a lawyer to advise me.

The problem with many excellent lawyers attending to Main Street business deals is that they know all about contract law but often much less about business. You have to weave and dodge as they fling bits of law at you. But what you really, really want to know is: what's the risk? Should I do the deal? If you ask them that question, they will typically offer a disclaimer to the effect that evaluating risk and reward in a transaction is not part of their job description.

I try to reduce my ignorance by talking to an accountant and visiting several lawyers, including a man I've known for over a decade. A knock 'em down fighter. Bright, quick, and arrogant. The never-ever-negotiate kind of lawyer. The Mike Tyson of law. We had talked recently and inconclusively. He took control of the meeting, of me, of the lease, as he does of everything and everyone around him. "We'll pull some money out of this deal, get you a driver," he assured me. "We'll fix 'em."

"A driver?" I say.

He nods affirmatively. He's one of the most knowledgeable and street-savvy business lawyers I know. A goose who refuses to lay his golden eggs in one sitting. He ushers me out, nodding at me knowingly, weighing my credits and debits, and coming up short.

I'm left to mull over his remark: *We'll get you a driver out of this.* What the hell was he talking about?

The next time I see Mike Lane and Bollinger I say: "Would you guys have any problem giving me a *driver*?" I think I'm using an auto-insider's jargon, all too cool, savvy. Why not an occasional chauffeur-driven car to escape having to drive in Seattle traffic? These auto guys have drivers to ferry high-value customers home while the dealership works on their cars.

"A driver?" Bollinger is astonished. Mike Lane takes a step back.

They look at me strangely. I must be a nutcase. Did I misuse the insider's lingo? The lawyer had used *driver* so expertly in his usual we'll-fix'em manner. I have the sense that I've said something wrong, mispronounced a word among the knowledgeable. Lane and Bollinger both start talking at once, and Bollinger finishes, "You mean a dealership demo car to drive?"

I realize my lack of knowledge. Dealers, key managers, and their spouses get to drive a free demo car. That's one of the benefits of owning and operating and working in management at a dealership. My toes curl from embarrassment. I must be blushing. They had thought I had wanted a chauffeur as well as a dealership loaner car to drive. Actually, so did I. I promise myself less bluff next time, more research.

The dialectics of deals are limited to the urgency of one or another detail, and by the presence or absence of competition. Connections matter. And there are different questions that have to be asked in each industry, but often you don't know what to ask. The conversations are sometimes stilted as each of the parties wait for the other to speak first.

By this time, I've talked to several general contractors, engaging each in a meeting, sometimes in follow-up meetings. The number of contractors I've talked to is probably excessive. But I'm gathering data and information, sometimes only flotsam and jetsam, as much as I can handle. Stick by beam, I'm becoming alert to greater complexity, the refined details, and the larger arena of facts a developer must learn. It costs contractors money to bid on this complex project. One builder has spent three months on preliminaries. He won't walk away easily. Still, I waffle when one of them asks me how many contractors are bidding. Who wants to learn that they have so much competition?

My writing aside, I'm preoccupied with choosing a contractor among competing contractors. I look for signs—whose background speaks to me? Whose outlook shows perseverance?

Though we're told to do otherwise, we do judge a book by its cover. And find it helpful. Typecasting is often the busy decision maker's refuge. Literary agents and publishers do it routinely. They have more manuscripts to read than the time or the will to read them. A bodice-ripper romance has a seminaked muscular man with a six-pack buff look, and smoldering eyes. This memoir has a picture of nineteen-year old Donna looking into the future of our uncertain life together. Publishing aside, I need an oracle to help me choose a contractor, but if the prescient deities are busy, I could use anything negative, an ugly rumor about one contractor so I can run to the other contractors.

To make my shopping among contractors more convincing, I take a leaf from Bollinger's book on optimism. Doubt doesn't sell. I'm ready to print a new business card: "Will Spend to Suit." The contractor I choose does four to six million dollars of contracting a year. I'm a big fish in his pond. What's made the decision firm is that the contractor knows one of the bankers who must sign off on my loan. This is a huge plus. Like hooking up with a literary agent who represents your best-selling teacher.

32

MY MEETINGS WITH BOLLINGER CONTINUE. WE SHAKE HANDS each time we meet as if to get in better touch with each other. We're becoming familiar, but not familiar enough to wave hello. If we're no longer strangers, we're semi-friends at best, connected as closely as two halves of a torn dollar bill. Undermining our appetite for risk is this awful fact: Bollinger's Lexus dealership may fail. If he can't pay the rent on his car palace, Donna and I can't pay the bank mortgage. Broke is no fun at any age, but going broke in midlife has its special terrors, like a bobsled flying off course that you can never retrieve.

But we're still winging it on smiles, accumulating mutual obligations, good intentions. I'm no longer the cool detached seller of land I had hoped to be. My writing is squeezed into tight mornings. Starting or owning a small business is never a good idea for the writer, and developing real estate isn't much better. The amount of mental energy a business requires obliterates much of everything else in the working day. Many writers choose odd jobs, freelance work with schedules they can control, wage stops between revisions, temporary work that doesn't corrupt the emotional space needed for writing. The fortunate ones get MFAs, teaching jobs, and time to write a book.

Donna and I do what we can to earn a living. Whenever her nerves are on edge, my writing suffers. The old cliché speaks of people being connected at the hip, which sounds awkward to me, but that might be the reason we hobble at times.

I secure a loan to finance Bollinger's car palace from a bank that has loaned me money before. That means I had started by querying second-and-third choice banks, learning on the move, spending my foolishness wisely before approaching my own bank. Now, to satisfy the bank, I'm looking for an independent appraiser to value the Lexus project "as built" before it's built. As everyone knows who's applied for a mortgage, this value has to be higher than the loan. My experience with appraisers is sketchy, but extensive enough to make me wary. Once I had fallen into unwanted ownership of a rental house, one that was turned over to me in settlement of claims for which I would have preferred to be paid in cash. I suppose the house could have been a palace in Bangladesh, a slum in Brooklyn, a derelict near a Florida swamp. In Seattle, however, real estate was hot. I sweated the cleanup yard work with Andrew's and Lisa's help. We crawled into narrow spaces underneath the porch to clean out debris. We cleaned under the eaves, and removed the moss from the roof, spruced up the backyard, painted a few rooms, and hauled away junk kept in the basement.

The appraiser found three Seattle houses dissimilar in one aspect or another he called "comps." Using the judgment all professionals must use, he decided that the house we wanted to use as collateral for a loan wasn't worth what I thought it should sell for. We were apart by thousands of dollars. "That's the way I see it," he said. He was Irish and the Irish are closer to God than the rest of us. I argued against the low value. He shook his head unburdened by doubt, and confirmed the appraisal with a tap of his college-ring finger. The sapphire stone flashed finality.

Unable to get the loan we needed because of the low appraisal, Donna and I sold the rental house at nearly thirty percent above the appraised value several months later. If this looks like a quirky process, it is. But no jumpier than starting new fiction.

I send Bollinger a timeline, a schedule of what I think should take place and when it should take place if he's to occupy the building in time. But when we meet there are new things said and unsaid as we face each other, silences wrought with ornate care. I'm not a happy developer. Selling was my first choice. I have visions of clever attorneys finding loopholes in any agreement we sign. Another banker I know, a backup not involved with my loan, says he wouldn't do it.

I ask Bollinger to initial the architectural drawings that my friend has drawn up. I hand him a soils report. I mention that the land has organic fill—tree stumps—that have to be removed and this may cause building delays, especially if it rains during construction, a good possibility in Seattle. I'm looking for transparency, overloading him with more information than he probably wants, or is used to getting. He's not a detail guy. I want to make sure he understands the risks. I don't want him complaining to me about cost overruns later.

How much more should I say? I ask him and Mike Lane to walk the perimeter of the lot again. We stand by the slick debris in the southeast corner. Their good leather shoes get mucked up. Bollinger looks up at the mountain of fill, the thick blackberry growth.

"This is it," I say and receive no response.

I see a site that's difficult to build on. The soils report has troubled me. The men who bore holes to inspect the soil are engineers, accustomed to tangible issues, specifics. The earth is beyond my influence. The land lies permanent, and geology is a science unmoved by salesmanship. The landfill will have to be removed for concrete footings to reach load-bearing soil.

Bollinger sees a grand dealership that will make him lots of money and advance him in the ranks of auto men. I point to the property line along a chain-link fence. A runoff from an unnamed culvert that goes dry in the summer now puddles small stagnant pools. They look at the wet jungle-like undergrowth with the uneasy distance of men used to shiny new things. I decide that I've done enough to show them the difficulties we might encounter.

At this point, the car palace venture had advanced far enough to see roads in the wood that diverged, allowing Donna and me to choose between two that are equally fair. We try to gauge the possibilities in our future—back to grad school, join the Peace Corps, start another business? The latter won't do, we realize. We're not particularly fit to run a business. We're searching for a way to reset and redirect our lives. But we still have the printing store that needs our attention. Once again the paper folder is rattling on with a sound approximating small arms fire. The images are all about conflict. We have to meet payroll and we don't have the money. Our finances remain precarious, good on paper without leaving loose change in our pockets. We tap into our line of credit.

33

BOLLINGER AND I ARE FINALLY DOWN TO THE LAST DETAILS of the build-to-suit lease. He's observant in many ways. But he deals in luxury and knows how to spend freely. Donna and I know how to be thrifty. Our financial acumen, what there is of it, lines up with an aversion to spending money needlessly. We have no desire for "pecuniary emulation" as described by Thorstein Veblen in *The Theory off the Leisure Class*, nor do we admire the "aestheticization of waste." Bollinger trusts us to be more cautious with expenses than he would be himself.

There's an escape clause in the lease for me. If the contractor's final bid for all the changes we require shoots far above our ongoing cost estimates, and I can't get additional bank financing, I may then cancel the deal and keep the advance money Bollinger paid for architectural and engineering work.

The final bids start coming in, startlingly higher than I expected.

There's no subtlety here, no nuance. The bid shows no facial ticks, no gestures, no hollowed-out eyes, or body language. I send the information to Bollinger on Sunday. I must have the lease revised once more before we sign off. On Monday I phone to ask if he's gotten it. He says he has. Yes, he's read it. He seems rushed, uncommunicative. I'd like to talk about it. "Thursday?" I ask.

I know instantly from the tone of his voice—the missing jovial laugh, the unhappy acknowledgement—that we've botched this relationship. He sounds as if he's been hijacked, and is speaking under duress. I feel my own stress. An inner tension muddles my thinking, brings on a confusion of roles—writer, businessman. The writer blunders toward the businessman, committing to paper my worries and wishes, some of which you've read here.

Words on paper have finality to them, a backbone. But doing deals is an oral craft. The paper and writing are there to document the ongoing action. I should have spoken to Bollinger earlier and handed him the letter afterward. Instead of engaging him in person over the phone or a cup of coffee, I wrote him a letter.

Perhaps we're both in over our heads.

After all the preliminaries—engineers, Lexus executives, architects, bankers, and city planners—I'm stunned by the final bids for the Lexus building. I need to persuade already-reluctant bankers to lend us more money on top of the fortune they've already promised. My enthusiasm fades, my lower back aches. We're approaching an amount twice our budget—a quantity of cash I can imagine only in drug dealers' hands—to build a building to sell a new product that might turn out to be the old Edsel. I'm getting cold feet.

Pressed to move forward or quit the project, I lose my feel for what I'm doing. If it's dealmaking, then every handhold and toe niche serves the climb. The rest is more tangled. Bollinger begs off on the meeting, claims to have too many meetings. He has a lease we had signed subject to several conditions, including my ability to secure a mortgage.

He wants the clock to run out, forcing me to go ahead with no more changes in the lease.

How urgent should I be with him? If he's to have his building completed by September we should meet in a minute. But the urgency isn't mine to keep—I pass it back to Bollinger. He backtracks and agrees to meet me. Thursday is fine; ten a.m. is all right. Our chances to have the building built in time are supremely thin.

We meet in his office, alone. He closes the solid-core door, a construction detail I've grown to appreciate when a contractor points out that the veneer-covered doors we had specified would not be in keeping with the quality of the Lexus building. We did a change-order for solid doors.

I sit on the tan leather couch, my favorite by now, the one closest to the exit. The furniture Bollinger had inherited four years earlier from the man who sold him the dealership is gone, along with the ceramic model of Queen Elizabeth II's coronation carriage and the delicate tea set that his predecessor had displayed.

Bollinger calls his advisers, Mike Lane, and a CPA, a man he has dealt with since his Walla Walla days. He asks the CPA to come up with another financial alternative. We go through the numbers. The two men leave to allow Bollinger and me to continue our private debate.

Bollinger remains restless, up from his chair, down again, swinging around, instinctively checking the showroom below, the customers, the salespeople, the walk-ins, the walk-outs, the deals in the making. His business instinct keeps him from folding quickly. He says we should go ahead with the building. We'll work out the details of the additional rent later. He stands again, making motions as if the meeting is over.

But without a change in the lease there's nothing to work out. I won't sign a construction contract. I hold a copy of the letter I had sent, eager to discover a way to sidestep our impasse. Bollinger checks his desk for something undone and then says, "I'm the world's worst negotiator."

He surprises me. Overconfidence is not one of my weaknesses. I've come expecting a man skilled, eager even, and more talented than me when it comes to commercial angles. I expect him to point out the rust in the trade-in I'm offering, a car without frills, many miles on the odometer. I expect a questioning assessment of the land I have owned for too long, the payments that drain my income. I expect to see a *Kelley Blue Book*, the industry bible of used car prices, whipped out from a vest pocket, with which he could reason with me, finishing with a sincere but low offer. Instead, I'm facing a man deeply disappointed, who says he's the world's worst negotiator.

"I need your Cadillac store to guarantee the lease," I say softly.

He doesn't hesitate this time, and says he'll pledge its stock, our main sticking point earlier. In a few sentences we've resolved the question and corralled the guarantee that's been running wild. But there's something more I need. His, and his wife's, personal signatures on the lease. No hiding behind corporations. He'll have to pledge all his assets to make the deal. Now we're thrown back to talking again about business being personal, or not. We're on Main Street, to me it's all personal. What he gets I lose, what he gives up I gain. But it's getting late. Bollinger impatiently says we can figure it all out later. I sense that he's throwing up his hands and needs to talk to his advisers again, in private. He calls them in.

Maybe the deal is off.

I excuse myself to let them speak privately, and wander among the automobiles in the showroom, feeling unsettled. You never know how far to go until you've gone too far. William Blake reminds us that "the road of excess leads to the palace of wisdom … you never know what is enough until you know what is more than enough."

Good advice for writers and business types alike. Without history to guide us, it's extremely difficult to see the damaging point of no return, and back off. Donna's and my experiences, though, and the many troubling stories of unfair business practices, make it harder for me to accept anyone's self-regarding business comments at face value.

I return to the meeting. Bollinger, trained in the enthusiasm of the sale, is restrained, observing me. His advisers have left. There's no mistaking what we are about. We're not talking about karma or Buddhism or the community of universal good spirits. We're not into altruism. There's no conflict between the practical and the spiritual. We're stoutly self-seeking guys defending our respective turf, and talking about who gets what and pays how much. It's the gimme-gimme-gotcha game, and we're playing it as best we know how. We're not anticipating Pope Francis's *Laudato si'* encyclical warning us: "If present trends continue, this century may well witness extraordinary climate change and an unprecedented destruction of ecosystems."

We want to make money. Simple. Direct. Personal. The economist Adam Smith would be pleased to see his "invisible hand" converting our hunt for personal gain into community benefit—hiring employees, contractors, paying for services, and real-estate taxes to support city and state. There's nothing of epic grandeur in what we're doing. All our energy is organized to win what we can from each other. Bollinger looks for an opening to charge through in my line of scrimmage. Could it be that D. H. Lawrence had a reason to claim that "The essential American soul is hard, isolate, stoic, and a killer."

I don't want to believe D. H. Lawrence. I listen to Bollinger. He says, "I could get you a partner for the real estate, but it's going to take time."

"I'll have to build the building without a partner to attract a partner?"

"That's right."

"But if you take a dive, no one will invest."

He doesn't answer. Looks away. Whatever our hopes, if his startup is *not* successful I won't find a partner, and if it's successful why do I need a partner to share the reward for the risk Donna and I take? Whoever is in charge of metaphysics and risk-analysis doesn't give enough thought to packaging risk. Like ketchup, it should come prepackaged in the bite-size portions fast food outlets hand out. After three packets of the stuff, I'm usually feeling guilty for the pile of waste next to the fries. However, risk comes every which way, and from every direction, and often it's camouflaged. "I don't think this will work out," I say. "I'm not going to spend a dime more unless we sign a longer lease. I'm done."

He smiles thinly. Riding a whiptail of emotion, he says, "Accusing you of bad faith probably isn't good enough to win a lawsuit." The truth is out once again: Our business friendship is as thin as paper. It needs a robust legal document that could withstand a lawsuit. He watches me carefully. I shake my head, feeling a rush of anger but I sit still. My voice drops a register, "Let's just forget it."

Bollinger is startled. He knows it's too late to restart the effort with another landowner. He must see what I feel. Emotion running high. The planes of my face intersecting in anger, the color rising. My cheeks stay warm. I point at the telephone. "You can call your lawyer right now." This isn't what he expected. We're not playing the usual reel-him-in sales game—first, you let the fish have a nibble, then you give the line a little jerk to set the hook, and then you …

We're slipping down a cascade, groping for a handhold. He catches himself first. "No, no, no," he says, "let's talk." The inner voice that rules such encounters allows me to accept his peace offering. We gang up on the missing lawyers, on lawyers in general. The agitation leaves me, and he offers a hesitant smile. "You should have told me you wanted more rent."

"I want a longer lease to amortize the building costs, not *more* rent."

"That sounds like more rent."

I don't argue the point. He would like the shortest lease possible, with many options to renew so he can get out quickly if his new dealership turns out badly. He wants to be free to abandon the building before it's paid for, leaving me with an empty special-purpose building I couldn't lease to anyone else at half the rent. But he also wants many options to extend the lease if he's making money. He wants all the cards in the deck. We sit at right angles and cross-purposes, arguing about the future neither one of us can foresee. I worry that the event unfolding between us might run amuck. And I worry that it might not unfold. He says he has to think it over before signing an amendment extending the term of the lease. We part, offering to get our lawyers in touch with each other, but we're uncertain if we have a deal or not.

34

THE PAPER FOLDER RUNS ON, MAKING A RACKET. DONNA'S part-time bookkeeper says the cash register is short fifty dollars. We hope it's nothing worse than one of our employees forgetting to ring up a void.

Donna takes a telephone call. "The airplane?" She sounds alarmed. She presses the phone fiercely against her ear and covers the other ear with her hand. More words are exchanged. She looks at me, her eyes ready to implode, her look harrowing. "I can't hear you," she says into the phone, her voice rising, tremulous. She calls out to me in Lithuanian.

"It's about Andrew!"

Our son, the boy who will grow up to be a firefighter and paramedic, is scheduled to return from a school trip overseas. He's taken by quick enthusiasms, by *Walden*, bicycles and soccer, by true love and by best friends—he's found more best friends in school than Donna and I would find in a lifetime. At seventeen he's also possessed by a suburban boy's passion for saving the environment, social justice, for girls, and for rap.

Donna is looking at me to do something.

"The plane?" I ask, holding my breath.

The insistent *shush clack clack* of the folder suddenly stops. I'm afraid of what she's is about to say. She looks distraught.

She sees my reflected terror and catches herself. "Andrew's all right. It's Bill on the phone." Bill is a parent who has a child attending the same school as Andrew. The earth is whole again, God forgiven. Our son is alive. I pick up the line. Bill apologizes for getting Donna upset. "They've closed down the airport," he says, his voice rising above the sound of the airport speakers. "Here, listen to what your son has done."

I take the phone. I imagine Bill holding the phone on its snakelike stainless steel cord of the payphone, aiming for the speakers in the ceiling so I could hear the announcement. I can barely separate the officious airport voice from the din in the background. Bill comes on the line again. "They're evacuating everyone from the south terminal."

Why do I need to know this? The afternoon was all right until now. I was happily preparing to attend another writers' conference.

"They found a bomb," Bill says. "The kids say Andrew packed it with his bike." He sounds perplexed. My heart skips a beat, seems to stop. I'm reduced to cautious mumbles. Thirteen students, my son and Bill's son among them, are returning from France. A few of the students have landed that day; Andrew is scheduled to return next week, but has shipped his bike ahead.

"You may want to get a lawyer before he gets back," Bill says.

Fear seizes me.

Bill puts his wife, who's a lawyer, on the phone. "Have you anyone in mind?" she asks.

I name a law firm I work with. The airport public address system asks passengers to evacuate the terminal. She says, "You don't need a real-estate lawyer, you need a *criminal* lawyer."

I struggle to understand. "I don't know of any." She offers two names. I'm amazed that she has the phone numbers handy. "They're both very good," she says. "They're probably leaving for the weekend. I'd call someone as soon as I could." I suspect she thinks I'm not catching on to the seriousness of my son being accused of hauling a bomb onto an airplane.

"There could be damages," she says. "Parents and passengers suing you for your son's actions."

I mumble my thanks.

Bill gets on the line and explains that the students are in the baggage-claim area looking for their bikes when a World War I artillery shell drops out of Andrew's bicycle carton. The attendant calls the Port of Seattle police, who call the bomb squad and a canine unit, the FBI, and the FAA. Four of the returning students are locked in an interrogation room. The parents are furious at the port police for not allowing them to speak to their children. Donna and I are not very happy either. The children, passengers and crew, our friend's child, could have been blown up midair by a war souvenir. I try a few words of apology.

The danger is past. No one is hurt. "We have all the TV stations here," Bill says, bemused. He's a banker uncomfortable with overstatement. Donna hovers at my elbow. She looks tired, but I know we're reflectors of each other. I'm not feeling chipper myself.

"I'll let you go," Bill says.

One of Donna's employees checks with a friend working at a TV station. His friend hears that the FBI is coming to question Donna and me. "No one's hurt," I say to reassure Donna. We leave immediately. I don't want to meet the FBI today, or tomorrow. I imagine two somber suited men of resolute politeness and slight humor. I check the rearview mirror every few minutes to see if an unmarked car is following us. I'm looking for a plain American car, a Ford, a Chrysler K-car, something from General Motors. In the space of a half hour we've been turned into fugitives.

No sirens sound at our arrival at home. My neighborhood looks unchanged. No TV crews, empty streets. No one on the drive and no one waiting by the front door holding handcuffs or a microphone displaying "KIRO 7 News." The phone rings as soon as Donna and I enter. We exchange glances, each expecting the other to answer the phone. I take it on the fourth ring.

"Mr. Trimakas?"

I'm beginning to notice how someone's politeness can make me edgy. It's a reporter from a local TV station. "I suppose you've heard?" She has an up voice. "Could I ask you a couple of questions?"

"I don't know anything," I plead, retreating from the quick friendship she's offering. I wonder how she's gotten my unlisted phone number.

"Our studio researcher says Andrew picked up an artillery shell at Verdun."

"I heard it was from World War I," I protest, looking for mitigating circumstances. The age of the shell makes it more of an antique, less of a crime. "A souvenir," I add, though I wish my son had taken to collecting plants and flower petals and pressing them in his notebook.

"I'm real close in Edmonds, Mr. Trimakas. Can I come over? It won't take but a few minutes."

I would buy Girl Scout cookies from a woman with her voice, she sounds so persuasive, but I can't see how this is going to help Andrew. Donna gives me anxious looks.

"I can't tell you anything," I say. My reticence, always healthy, grows larger. "We don't know anything."

"Are you sure we can't come over?"

I've heard the plural. The reporter isn't alone. A cameraman is with her.

I imagine pictures of distraught parents on TV, the worried mother, stunned father. *How does this make you feel?* the reporter would be asking. *The plane could have been blown out of the sky.*

"It won't take much time," she says.

It turns out that the reporter's daughter goes to the same school as my son. "Look, I'm sorry. I don't want to be on TV," I say.

"Will you talk to one of the other stations?"

I assure her that she won't be scooped. She finally gives up.

I call another lawyer I know. The man is irritated that my intense tone had gotten me past his secretary late on a Friday afternoon. I tell him the FBI is looking for my son. He hears me out impatiently.

"Ed, maybe it's a good thing."

"A good thing? The worst he's done is t.p. a neighbor's evergreen last Halloween. The boy is going to be hauled off to jail and you call that a good thing?"

"Teach him a lesson."

"I don't want him to have a lesson in jail."

"They've got to learn sometime."

I hang up.

Donna and I fidget and nervously eat potato chips. We call our real-estate lawyer, a remarkably skilled woman, always helpful, eternally competent, and tell her what's happened. She also says we need a criminal lawyer and gives us a name to call.

"Next week when Andrew gets back?" I ask.

"No, no! You need the lawyer *before* Andrew sets foot in this country. You need a lawyer to talk to the authorities. Otherwise he'll be arrested the minute he steps off the plane."

I call the lawyer she recommends and leave a message.

We wait for the local news, wait for the FBI, wait for a call from France from our son. We place outgoing calls on one line and take incoming calls on another. We're waiting on several lawyers to call us back. Coffee cups lie about. Had we not stopped smoking years earlier, the house would now reek of cigarette smoke. I can't help wondering if our phone has been tapped.

One of the criminal lawyers returns my call. He's heard about the airport closing, but his schedule won't allow him to take another case. I weigh the voices, the phone manners. I'm looking for a defender, a confidant, a fighter against superior government forces organized to jail my son.

The local news comes on. The airport closing is the main story on all three networks. Cable news isn't yet the big thing it will become. I flip impatiently from one channel to the next, looking at video images of parents, sweaty under the TV lights and angry with the Port Authority for keeping them away from their children.

The jump-cut editing is quick and compelling. We see a bomb squad working, then a receding shot of a fifty-five-gallon barrel loaded on a flatbed truck as it heads for Fort Lewis. A TV reporter ominously explains that a bomb had been *smuggled* onto the plane. I despise the man for his choice of words. My son was certainly foolish, but not a bomb smuggler.

There's a heightened sense of reality and unreality, a hallucinatory drama much more exciting than the rusty object that's been shown on the screen. The cuts and fades and sound bites, shiny, bright-eyed faces, distraught students hanging limply together, weeping and fearful after their confinement and interrogation. A portly officer ill at ease in the sudden limelight takes a browbeating from one of the parents.

The other lawyer finally reaches us. I worry that Andrew might be railroaded in some fashion, made an example, used for a teachable civic moment, then handcuffed. My fear of authority seems rampant, excessive. The lawyer explains that a district attorney has to file charges. She talks about the circumstances. Andrew is a minor. There was no intent. They're pretty busy these days with real terrorists. She'll find out if the district attorney is interested in doing anything.

"Doing anything? Doing what?"

"If the district attorney passes on it, then we don't have a local criminal problem but a civil one that doesn't necessarily disappear. But then we have the feds. The FAA takes jurisdiction. If the FAA doesn't take jurisdiction, the Tobacco and Firearms people might. They're known as the federal judiciary scavengers. I don't think the Port Authority people are interested, but you never know."

"My kid is in France. What if the French police pick him up?"

"That could be a problem."

I tell her I'm waiting for the FBI. But the bureau has no hold on her imagination as it does on mine. She calmly tells me to inform policing authorities that Andrew is represented by counsel, and to refer them to her.

I'm ambivalent about lawyers. I like them and avoid them whenever I can. I like them socially and over a good lunch. I like them more if they're mine. I like lawyers who become judges. I like constitutional scholars and public defenders, and most recently I like Andrew's criminal lawyer, Kate. This client schizophrenia is something that experienced lawyers accept without much wasted emotion.

Donna takes the next call and hands me the phone. A man's sharp voice announces he's a special agent for the FAA. I don't ask him how he's gotten our unlisted phone number.

"You must be pretty worried about what's going on," he says, setting me back with unexpected kindness. I tell him I know nothing more than what I've heard on the news: that Andrew had picked up a souvenir, a loss to other boys who might have found the shell equally compelling.

The agent says he has a teenage son. He volunteers to keep us informed, and gives us his home phone in case we want to talk to him over the weekend. Suddenly I love authority, government officials helping citizens. But my mind flips over to suspicion. Is this a setup? What game is this man playing?

"When is Andrew coming back?" he asks.

"Next week," I say, realizing that it doesn't look good that his souvenir took an earlier flight while he remained in Paris.

"We're going to detonate it at Fort Lewis and see if it's live," the agent says. This man sounds so calm. I would like him to be on *my* plane in case of a hijacking.

"What if it's a dud?"

"That would be good," he says. "There's no fuse in the nose, so the shell isn't armed. The explosives have a tendency to crystallize over time and become highly unstable." He tells me that the FBI has its mind set on terrorism. The FAA agent doesn't see it in the same light. I'm grateful.

35

THE RADIO, THE NEWSPAPERS, AND THE TV STATIONS HAVE reported our son's bomb scare. Even the French press has gotten in on the news. I have the odd sense of being a local scandalous celebrity. The irate letters to the editor have started coming in, mostly the teach-the-dumb-kid-a-fucking-lesson kind. A passenger delayed by the airport closing claims emotional trauma and threatens to sue our son's school and us.

There are things out in the world that will eat you, or tear you apart. My brother and I used to collect shrapnel, brass casings, odd-smelling phosphorescent charges that blew up on contact with water—the detritus of war scattered over Europe when I was a child. Not once did we volunteer to share our found treasures with our parents. My brother was no radical, and I was too young to be anything but curious. Looking back on our hunt for explosives, it's a wonder he lived to become a priest, and I still have both hands.

Our real-estate agent calls to ask what's happening. I tell him I'm working on it. I don't know much about cars, less about dealerships, and nothing about keeping a kid out of jail. What I surrender to inexperience I try to recover through research, diligent work. I also bluff on occasion, muck about, stumble, and question my way into an answer, scouring the vast unknown for scraps of knowledge.

Between unsuccessful overseas calls to trace Andrew's whereabouts and Parisian telephone operators unwilling to put up with my garbled French, I find that the world goes on as it normally does, indifferent to our needs. The FAA agent calls me again. "The shell was live," he says in a deadpan voice. He explains that the case is out of his hands until the district attorney decides if he wants to try Andrew on criminal charges.

The Bollinger venture, the novel, the writers' conference, the printing store, the accumulation of all that was passionately important and hotly contested just a few days ago fades into insignificance. I ask the FAA man how they came to their conclusion. He says that ordinance specialists at Fort Lewis first estimated the size of fragments that would result from detonating a measured plastic explosive attached to the side of the shell and if the resulting fragments were smaller, they assumed the shell must have been live. An iffy science it seems to me, considering that no one can say how old the shell is, nor identify it as German or French.

"The fragments were smaller than estimated," the FAA man says.

I want to tell him that they've blown up the evidence, but I remain silent. I call the lawyer I had hired for Andrew and ask if I should cancel the flight to the writers' conference the following weekend. She says she'll let me know.

A second letter arrives at my son's school from the distressed passenger. He claims that the two-hour bomb scare had so frightened him that it adversely affected his health. He wants Andrew to write an essay of penance graphically describing the maiming and mutilation of bodies blown apart at thirty-thousand feet.

The man threatens to sue once more. Our lawyer says to us, "Don't talk to anyone. And for God's sake, don't *write* anything."

Our son, it turns out, hauled a heavy, muddy, corroded WWI artillery shell over cobblestoned streets in a bicycle pannier for three weeks without it exploding. His classmates had even tossed it around. They dropped it once and thought nothing of it. The school trip was an experiment in student self-rule. Laissez-faire was working. The students didn't seem to mind an ugly projectile, but surely a teacher, one of the two adults in charge, should have been more aware, alert to the danger of a projectile removed from a battlefield.

I push away the thought. The teachers had never seen military service, and none of the students had any idea what danger they were courting. As one student said, they've not been trained in munitions. And who can fathom the depths to which an inquisitive teenage mind might pursue his curiosity?

Good news arrives. We get a phone call from Andrew. He's safe, and has a plane ticket home. With our son located, the lawyer engaged, the media hounds focused elsewhere, and the FBI into larger challenges, the district attorney lets Andrew's lawyer know that they're not interested in prosecuting. This good news allows me to settle into the mildly euphoric and anticipatory bubble of going to a writers' conference—a wonderful high that usually lasts for a month or two after the conference.

I enjoy the technical problems a book presents, the form, one event pushed against another, the structure—what precedes and what follows to keep a reader engaged, the pacing, a path to the end, and the craft to get it all together. Katherine Anne Porter offers encouragement: "Practice an art for love and the happiness of your life. You will find it outlasts almost everything except breath."

My purpose for attending the conference is both clear and murky. I check into the conference hotel thinking that God must have had a great time those first days in Genesis. In the beginning was the word, which might help explain why there are so many creative writing programs, workshops, conferences, seminars, readings, and manuscripts floating around.

Wittgenstein says that words and language limit our universe. I'm inclined to believe this, though other senses come into play. Are the words *mystery, ineffable, infinite, indefinable, unknowable, liminal* merely words or do they point beyond words? Writings remain a mystery until written, an act shrouded by the limitations of intellect, language, sensibility, receptivity, and experience.

But how to say it well is a wonderful skill.

The skill comes from writing, not from talking about writing. The same advice applies to business. You learn business by doing business. Practice is the teacher, failure the dean. That said, there are many good reasons to persist with one's writing beyond an ambition to have a career. It's a life-giving lifelong engagement with the creative challenge of discovering others and yourself, perhaps even defining yourself, advancing lines of emotion, uncovering limits to knowledge, exploring the ways people and methods and culture work together, or fall apart.

At the conference, we discuss the merits of epiphanies, the weakness of endings, the lightness of being. I straddle two workshops, one for nonfiction and the other for fiction writers. I look in at one workshop and attend the other, or vice versa. Some part of my nature says I should have stayed at home writing (or dealing with Bollinger.) But the socially inclined part wants to meet intelligent, many-talented, and passionate writers. De Tocqueville long ago described the American penchant for association. For the most part, I had a good time going to workshops. That starts me to thinking about returning to graduate school for an arts degree as a counterweight to the MBA I'd earned. But mostly I want to improve my writing skills, along with my slack knowledge of literature.

Once again Donna gives me a questioning look.

Delmore Schwartz was famous at twenty-six. William Styron was acclaimed at twenty-six as well. Updike rocketed in the literary world from his early twenties. Norman Mailer was world famous at twenty-five. Joan Didion and other talented writers had a youthful career booming. F. Scott Fitzgerald, Ernest Hemingway, Flannery O'Connor, and countless celebrated writers launched their careers before breaking thirty.

Prior to the mid-twentieth century none of our writers went to school to learn to write. The reliably resourceful David Mamet, ever the iconoclast, has observed that going to school teaches one to obey, follow rules, and accept received conventions, some of which may be damaging to creative spirits. Likewise the great English poet William Blake, the creator of a stunning imaginative world, scorned formal education: *Thank God I never was sent to school / To be flogged into following the style of a fool.*

But in the absence of salons or family engaged in the creative arts, school is one place to find association with artists. And there's something else, too. The post WWII immigrant children of European parents like me—displaced so many times, all our possessions lost, the privileges of the middle class and professional callings aborted—often value education beyond its practical career potential. It was the only thing that we carried that was truly portable. Short of murder, neither the fascists nor communists could take your education away, not by whim nor by club.

Writings, too, are portable. Samuel Johnson says, "the only end of writing is to enable the readers better to enjoy life, or better to endure it." And reminds us that "no man but a blockhead ever wrote except for money."

Johnson's advice aside, traditionally published writers and independently published writers mostly live within a perilous artist "gift" economy

(Lewis Hyde, *The Gift*) joined by poets, gardeners, painters, musicians, actors, dancers, artists, and craftspeople of many varieties who work for little or no money to create and practice what pleases them, with the hope that it pleases others willing to pay for such pleasure. Only two percent of writers claim to earn a living from their writing. A 2015 Authors Guild survey reports that the majority of its authors, privileged to have a traditional publisher's contract, would be living under the federal poverty level if they depended solely on income from their writing.

What's the lesson here?

James Baldwin says in his *Paris Review* interview: "Find a way to keep alive and write. There is nothing else to say. If you are going to be a writer there is nothing I can say to stop you ..." If some of that writing is rewarded by commerce, so much the better. Write at your own risk. It's a noble effort.

36

A T THE PRINTING STORE, WE'RE NOT INTO HIRING HIGHBORN candidates. We're hiring people to serve customers. My job is to thin the ranks and preselect the most promising people for Donna to see. A question on our application asks, "Have you ever been fired?" The friendly man I'm interviewing answers yes. A point in his favor, he's honest.

Truth, though, has its limits. When Donna and I were desperate for income after one of our near-bankruptcies, she applied for work as a clerk at a big-box store. Faced with the question "Have you ever taken anything that wasn't yours?" she favored the literal over the metaphorical and answered yes. She was eight or nine years old when she took a glass marble she had found on the street, and this innocent taking somehow blazed in her memory over a lifetime. Maybe she was thinking of George Washington. In any case, Big Box didn't hire her.

I ask our candidate about the circumstances of his firing. He says he was fired for being incompetent. I'm taken aback, and then I think, aren't all of us incompetent at one task or another at some point in our lives?

"You were incompetent?" I ask.

"I didn't know how to do the work."

I dither over how to continue. Without mentors—the situation most of us face—we're on our own. A few stars flare early, and we welcome them, the brightness, the hope, literary and otherwise, even if most of us have to wend our way around the skies unnoticed. "Was it lack of training?" I ask.

"Yeah, more than I could handle."

Emo isn't this man's style. He's experienced, and applying for a job as a printing-press operator. He shows me excellent samples of his printing. I shuffle the man's application from one hand to the other. The candidate looks to me to be about thirty years old. "You were how old when you were fired?"

"Seventeen."

God help everyone of us who have to be judged in adult life on how we were at seventeen. The man started to work for us the following week.

The car palace venture is smoldering like a damp campground fire just before it might blaze. Bollinger arranges an interview with his then-wife for my book. I'm on Mercer Island, a privileged place where some of the wealthiest in the Seattle metropolitan region live. The houses here are priced well above the median price of homes anywhere, and as much as ten or twenty times above the price of a house where Bollinger wants me to build his Lexus dealership.

If no man is an island unto himself, many residents here argue the opposite. A working man could work several lifetimes and the sum of all those years of work would not be enough to afford him a house on the shoreline idealized in Seattle as "waterfront property."

Bollinger's wife opens the door. She's a slim, attractive woman. She says that her part-time housekeeper has the day off, and directs me toward a cream-colored living room. I take my tape recorder with me, though I'm still not used to the small buttons.

A mother, a spouse, an independent woman, she tells me of the friends they've kept, a number from their Walla Walla days, some of them now divorced. She met him on a lark, on a friend's dare. They fell in love and married three months later. Their life together has been centered on raising a family of five children. Two of hers and three of his. I see him as the optimistic businessman. She sees her husband as the man who brings home a briefcase of work at night. She talks about traveling with him on business trips, mainly so that they can find the time to be together.

I mention their generous donation to the Seattle Symphony. "Does he like classical music?" It's a loaded question, because I suspect he doesn't. She won't say if he likes, or dislikes, classical music. She says that such high-culture, high-profile donations help sell a luxury product. My tax-deductible contributions look pallid in comparison, small donations to the American Civil Liberties Union and Amnesty International. Donna donates to Doctors Without Borders, and every pet and animal healing effort that can get her attention.

"What's your book about?"

I avoid a direct answer, moving on to another question. I'm a novice interviewer. Years earlier I did an extremely short gig as a reporter, working for the wage of a byline at a publication that soon went out of business. In several instances of working on *Car Palace*, I'd forgotten to turn on the recorder, and at other times I didn't have it with me. I'm learning how to arrange facts and local color worth reporting, gathering details, looking for the obscure revelation, the catchy quote, the human interest, but I feel I'm merely nosy. I'm not used to the reporter's persistence, nor do I have the requisite inquisitive boldness many journalists display. In fact, I feel like an overly polite intruder.

Politeness is not the attitude that corrals breaking news stories. Bob Woodward wouldn't have felt that way, nor Janet Malcolm or Jane Mayer, who gave us the riveting *Dark Money* exploration of the billionaire class. (Upset by her revelations, they hired investigators to denounce her, a scenario that was played out decades earlier when General Motors hired spooks to investigate Ralph Nader.)

Geoffrey Wolff says I must put aside my reservations about writing about Main Street commerce. Human experience, even how deals are made, can be interesting. I have argued in this memoir that the patterns of venturing in business and creative writing have broad similarities. I've shown how Donna and I embraced our dazzling blindness by working our way across an unfamiliar landscape on a path to an unknown future. *Car Palace* offers an antidote to the current fascination with megawealthy individuals, their possessions, private jets and islands and spending habits. What's often elided is their epic neediness and insatiable, compulsive, cunning energy to stay on top. Few writers start their careers with an inheritance, as most of the superwealthy do.

The short stories and essays discussed at workshops offer few clues to anyone's ability to go the length of a book. I start, as most writers do at these workshops, unbidden, knowing that no one invites us to write. For most writers I know, the process is chaotic, juggling paragraphs, scenes, and chapter-length sections. I might write a beginning near the end of the story, throw the middle out, discard a number of titles, rewrite ten endings, and write myself into a vapor to find peace with what I've written.

I'm told that neither Isaac Asimov nor the British writer Anita Brookner had to rewrite a word once written. I envy them. Gabriel

García Márquez, in the late portion of his dazzling career, designed a plot, a narrative arc. His earlier books were not plotted. He wrote his way into the final version by expansive rewriting. John Irving, a consummate professional, can't begin writing a story without knowing the title. Every piece of advice offered by one successful writer could find another successful writer offering opposing advice. Some writers say that you can't begin a story until you have the first sentence, some say that you can't start until you have the ending figured out, and most everyone says that, like god, the writer must know everything.

Some observers believe that creativity must come to us in one vivid, grand insight, and sometimes perhaps it does, perfectly formed as Athena born out of the brow of Zeus. For the most part, this isn't true of creative projects.

It's troubling to imagine Homer scratching out lines, substituting words, equivocating over meanings, and adding marginal comments as he composes one or another oral epic. But Homer had centuries of Homeric assistants and thousands of years of oral tradition to polish his stories. This pedestrian approach, many hands at the helm, or at least many tries navigating, is also foreign to my thoughts about Shakespeare. But scholars have shown that Shakespeare was a working writer who could be disappointed with a theater audience's reaction to a scene and go home to rewrite a scene to make it better in the next performance.

The "creative genius" argument saddles those of us who wish to create something with an immense fear that if we can't see the perfect whole before starting, it may escape us forever. This fear, in business, in writing, in life, forces many of us not to make an attempt.

But many of us have seen x-rays of old masters' paintings showing clearly the pentimento, where an arm, a head, feet and fingers, may have been positioned badly, repositioned, even repeatedly, and painted over. The maquettes made by Degas—some were accomplished, some stilted—and the sketches by Renoir, or the preliminary small-scale scenes drawn by Rubens, all show the same trial-and-error effort applied to creating a masterpiece. And if you're a writer, you may have read *The Paris Review* interviews, showing the annotated manuscripts being revised. Even one of the most celebrated memoirs of our time, Vladimir Nabokov's *Speak, Memory* was first offered as *Conclusive Evidence* and revised fifteen years later.

It seems to me that very little of the world's cache of good work was created with one perfect, original vision, an encouragement to those of us who would gratefully try many times.

The problem with books and with business remains: Both are made of many parts, several middles and many beginnings. Which part should come first is the usual question but the wrong one to ask for creative people wanting to break the narrow confines of serial thinking.

Regarding Lexus—two, three, maybe four strands of the venture were launched at once. The bankers, appraisers, engineers and city planners engaged all simultaneously even as quarrels over the lease continued. Did we know that the strands would twine together and form a string? No, but we hoped they would.

Once a thing is done, it's easy to see how to do it again, provided the variations are limited. That's true of many business efforts—repeating a success three times, four times, a hundred thousand times over. Repeating a successful formula often makes businessmen and businesswomen wealthy, and it makes them often boring. The repetitive, linear approach is not how artists like to think. They often prefer not to do the same thing twice.

Having your ducks lined up in a row is also a great idea, but parallel lines of work with a single goal in mind is the more likely approach. Words must be arranged one after another, but the characters, the themes, the scenes born of chaos, the beginnings, the hardness of your material, the polish, the grain, the size and the form, are not done one after another but often simultaneously. Few writers hew a story out of stone in one step, and few businesspeople get it right on the first try. You must be willing to start with many items unresolved, adjusting your work as you progress without being terrified that the loose ends won't bind together—sometimes they don't.

In *How to Write a Novel*, John Braine, who also wrote the novel *Room at the Top*, has some good advice on the subject. He says one should write heedless of editorial thoughts, the questioning, the punctilious grammar and nuanced word. He suggests a conscious steady flow, moving too quickly for barnacles of doubt to attach themselves before the first draft is finished. In his congenial and helpful book he acknowledges that there are countless ways to proceed, but he favors his approach.

The effort often produces much unusable material: autumn leaves left from seasons past, a clutter here, a pile along the fence line, a scattering across the street. But even as the stuff accumulates, it calms the most innermost worry: "Do you have enough material to revise for a book?" Sometimes you don't. Sometimes it's best to condense what you have into a magazine article. But what better proof than pages added every day? Thoughts released in a flood can be brought to discipline later. A vacuum, a blank page, offers nothing. So the process is clumsy, really it is. So many chapters abandoned, wrecks along a serpentine road.

As I leave Bollinger's house, his wife walks me outside and we say goodbye. She doesn't turn away but backs up, stepping backward, eyes lit, edging toward the safety of the front door. "Treat us kindly," she says.

37

O UR SON REMAINS UNDER INVESTIGATION. AN FBI AGENT reports that his classmates said that he took the Verdun shell against his teacher's permission. This is not what I hear from Andrew.

I don't want to be the father who kills Santa Claus, darkens the virtues of friendship. Nonetheless, I say, "I don't think their story is helping you." There's a life lesson here, somewhere. I hope Andrew is getting it. Friendships aren't made of steel, one might say marriages too. Both are made of trust, but circumstances change, emotions fade, attentions wander, new people walk into your life. Can trust handle it all?

There is something else here—a lesson in police powers. Authorities can coerce statements and confessions without using whips, without waterboards, without applying electric prods or zapping Tasers. The FAA agent tells me that the FBI is making too much of Andrew's bomb incident. I imagine the police being impatient interrogators, as I might be impatient seeking results at work, an impatience that's useful to motivate action, but dangerous to our freedoms if exercised by the police and prosecutors acting too quickly as judges.

Andrew's classmates were all best friends until they were interrogated. I visualize the room where their questioning took place. Bare, sharp lighting, utilitarian furniture. Two FBI agents, two or three Port of Seattle police, an FAA agent, perhaps an airline representative, and four returning teenagers. The students are exhausted from twenty hours of airports, of flight and boredom from so much sitting. Not one of them has slept a full night in five. The locked airport room is the closest any of them will come to sitting in prison. They feel coerced into "keeping the story straight."

This touch of paranoia in me, the John Kennedy Toole persona from *A Confederacy of Dunces* brings back to my mind the cop who wanted to teach me a lesson when I was about twelve or thirteen. I was an accomplished box rider—the vehicle of choice among urban street kids before skateboards arrived.

You take apart a metal rollerskate and nail one half to the front of a piece of lumber, usually a two-by-four about four feet long and the other half to the rear to build your moving platform. Then you nail a grocer's discarded wooden vegetable crate to the front of your foot-propelled vehicle, and if you liked handlebars you could screw down two small pieces of wood to the top of the crate, but most of us just held on to the crate. You step on board with one foot, and kick away with the other. This wasn't quite the raft that Huck Finn rode, but it was my version of freedom adapted to Brooklyn sidewalks.

Someone must have reported suspicious neighborhood activity, and the cop who came to investigate finds me a touch too suspicious. "Come here," he says, eyes flashing authority.

I come forward. "Sir?" I say.

He demands to know what I'm doing.

"Sir?"

Did I say something wrong? Meanings sometime wandered off unintentionally. Before I learned colloquial English, I used to think that kids my age yelling "shuddup" were calling each other "pig"—which would have worked interchangeably with "shut up," given our juvenile excitement.

In any case, the officer pulls me by my shirt collar. I try to make myself little. He whips my face with his leather gloves, and tells me to scram—a blow that I've never forgotten, or forgiven.

My sense of intrigue, and the occasional edginess I feel toward authority, the curse of displaced refugees growing up among many dangers, the fear of a person not assured of a permanent place by birth, remains. Documented, yes, naturalized—thank you—and gratefully living with the gift of citizenship bestowed on me by my fellow citizens.

Andrew, his lawyer Kate, the FAA agent and I are in the top reaches of the Smith Tower, once Seattle's and the West's tallest building. It's an overcast day. The sky and the bay are united in a murky arrangement of grays. Andrew is silent. He doesn't appear nervous. But he must be. His lower chin has broken out in a juvenile archipelago of "zits," as he calls them.

I'm not inclined to believe that the best outcomes, the most impartial and equitable, the win-win situations that we like to talk about, always prevail. I've taken sides in Andrew's FAA investigation. My son's side. If he has to be hurt by legal proceedings, I'd rather see a small injury. I'm the parent wishing that his bold child suffers a tumble that will make him more careful in the future.

Once again I wonder if he has been raised too sheltered, as if my own anxious upbringing in Brooklyn had prepared me better. Stepping out of a subway station near my home I would pause to see which side of the street offered safe passage home. Children growing up in the suburbs see college admissions and SAT scores arc across their experience with the fierceness of gangs we otherwise only read about. A youth growing up in a cozy, safe environment can be forgiven for thinking that everyone has a good heart, and could be a friend.

Kate sits at the head of the table. She doesn't have to say more than she has to remind me that advocacy comes in two parts, saying the right things and not saying the wrong things. Silence is a tool. We can't afford to be reckless, even with truth.

I keep mostly quiet and pay attention to the way the agent phrases his questions, the way he leans forward. He seems sympathetic. This meeting may have several outcomes. It all depends on what Kate will allow Andrew to say, and how he says it, and what the agent investigating thinks.

I asked Donna not to come.

We don't want parental emotions intruding on an inquest we hope will clear Andrew of malicious intent.

The man questioning him is part bureaucrat, part activist, and a federal agent. He has a deep scar on his neck, a man with an edge. I would have liked to have had him with me in my youth, walking me home from the subway station.

He has investigated Andrew's school; he has interviewed Andrew's headmaster, his teachers, and a few students. He's walked the brick and ivy courtyard, seen the sheltered educational enclave of privileged youth, the absence of danger, the abundance of common sense. "I have to ask this," he says. "Do you now belong to, or have you ever have been a member of, Hezbollah?"

Andrew repeats the name Hezbollah, garbling it a little.

"A fundamentalist Muslim terrorist group," I say.

Andrew recoils. "I've never heard of them."

The FAA agent doesn't play politics. Terrorists come equipped with a range of beliefs. Domestic terrorists have shot dozens of gay victims, bombed abortion clinics, federal buildings, and murdered doctors. The agent is going by his script. I can see him in an elite corps of fighters, but he would be more articulate than most, and much quicker.

He asks if Andrew belongs to a white supremacist group and gets the same hesitant, surprised denial. Andrew and the agent are getting into the details of his souvenir when Kate interrupts. "You thought it was a shell casing and on top the thing for gunpowder?"

Andrew says, yes. The agent looks surprised.

"I thought it was like the shell from a rifle," Andrew says.

Kate prods, "Are you talking about the bullet, or the part that holds the gunpowder?"

"Not the bullet," Andrew says. He has composed himself into stillness.

"A cartridge! You're talking about the cartridge," Kate says. "A mud-filled cartridge." She turns to the agent, "He didn't even *know* that it was potentially explosive."

The World War I shell is blunted and rectangular in profile. The *mot juste* escapes us as we look for distinctions between a cartridge and shell. Kate, though, is pleased by this renewed demonstration of Andrew's lack of ordinance knowledge. It helps his defense.

Later, I check with Donna's brother, a retired Army colonel. He says we're talking about a round, a projectile. His sources say the round had exploded, sizzling like a wet firecracker. Slow ignition, he called it. The FAA agent hadn't told us this. In effect the bomb was a dud. Was our agent misinformed? Did he mislead us? The souvenir was less dangerous than we'd thought. Nonetheless, officials are working to keep us safe.

38

DONNA AND I HAVE FITTED TOGETHER A NUMBER OF PIECES toward the completion of our Bollinger venture. Still missing is the signed lease extension carefully crafted by our real-estate lawyer. I consider calling the architect to tell him to stop work. I call Bollinger instead. "I can't go on," I say. "I need a longer lease to recover the enormous cost of building your Lexus dealership." We meet at Denny's and wrangle some more. We're also trying to stay nice with each other.

I hesitate a moment, wondering if I should add humor by mentioning to Bollinger that in my once youthful proximity to things I could never own, I identified a Cadillac emblazoned with glittering extravagance as a Pimpmobile.

I decide on discretion by censoring myself.

Instead, I tell him that Donna and I had a Cadillac connection lurking in our background. This sparks his interest. I tell him about our Abbey Carpet stores. Our plunge into the retail carpet carnival had landed us among a flamboyant group of people whose vehicle of choice was the Cadillac. The franchise operations manager drove a Cadillac, the executive director, the franchise director, the merchandising manager, most of the sales trainers had Cadillacs, and of course the president and founder of the company, the much-admired Milt Levinson, drove a dark burgundy model.

Levinson was way beyond the staid corporate ladder I'd been climbing, which was part of his great charm. Though Jewish, he named his chain Abbey and chose a jovial Franciscan abbot for his company logo. The rotund abbot blended the mendicant, the meditative and the mercantile. How could Donna and I resist? We were getting a lesson in the mutability of imaginative thinking, the flexibility of forms, the allure of arresting symbols, signs and images. The Cadillac message was not subliminal either. It tantalized, it begged, it bragged, it even shouted: Join us to own your own Cadillac! We did.

This led to our first wholesale furniture mart. The Mart, as it's known, is where retailers of furniture, case goods, soft goods, home furnishings and carpet come to inspect manufacturers' seasonal product offerings. There's one in Chicago, another in San Francisco, one in Atlanta, and in Seattle. The Chicago and San Francisco Marts are two of the largest.

We're in San Francisco. It's winter. Donna wears the clothes appropriate to her profession, a teacher loyal to the conservative fashion of her third-graders. I wear a three-piece suit, my corporate inheritance. I look somewhat geeky among the open-collar, tieless, profane, heavy gold-chain wearing men. We didn't have the word *bling* early on, but this conference provided bling bling bling. The gold chains resplendent, the women outspoken. A production of *Hair* was making a successful nationwide tour, and high-school seniors were singing about the "Age of Aquarius" to entertain Rotarians.

After years of polishing my subdued corporate look, flamboyant was in. Enough of violins, I said to myself, let's go for percussion, timpanis, cymbals and trumpets and French horns. Donna and I were dealers now, sudden members of a new fraternity, the effervescent, the optimistic, and the loud.

We advertised "doorbuster" sales for installed wall-to-wall carpet, free credit, deluxe pad, living room, dining room, and hall. The installation was guaranteed for the life of the carpet. We worked every three-day holiday weekend and made house calls to sell to homeowners after they would return from work—seven and eight and nine in the evening.

The iconic Abbey abbot, the company's chief salesman, smiled extravagantly, happy to be seen in our TV and print ads, letting shoppers know we had carpeted the homes of the stars: Ida Lupino praised it, her husband Howard Duff loved our carpet, and Anne Francis, a star in *Forbidden Planet* and *Blackboard Jungle*, loved it, too.

The camaraderie of the Mart echoes in the hallways, turns louder in the carpet showrooms. "Naw, for God's sake, not *that* one. Your *mother* won't buy it at wholesale!" The men outnumber the women. They talk about "cherry-picking" the best lines, buying the "crème de la crème."

I work to fit myself into the Cadillac-driven mercantile consciousness and leave the geeky vest of my three-piece suit in the hotel-room closet. I loosen my tie. The cocooned low-decibel corporate buzz I experienced with my former employers is in the past. I like the satisfying sound of big-ticket retail commerce, of industrial and merchant knowledge passed hand to hand, laugh to laugh.

That evening Donna and I enjoy another ritual—the soiree—Mohawk Carpet is hosting a dinner to thank dealers for selling its product. The Italian restaurant is located in a North Beach cellar. With nearly eighty people jammed inside it's not only warm, but also intimate with fellowship. The drinks are served with extravagant freedom; the food is ample and fresh. Cigarette and cigar smoke curls, twines, and thickens in a dozen scents. The alcohol encourages retail anecdotes, ribald laughs, intimate asides about this or that huge merchandise mistake, of one or another misalliance.

I never knew that carpet could be so much fun.

My head buzzes to a frequency adjusted to Johnnie Walker. Donna is extraordinarily bright-eyed, too. We're profitable franchisees, less inclined to bicker with the franchiser, a persuasive man of immense mercurial energy and strong direction. He had negotiated a lease for us near a regional mall in Seattle; a long lease with many options, a lease I wouldn't have had the knowledge, clout, or experience to nego-tiate. His company guaranteed our creditworthy performance on the lease—a lease that would eventually earn us a small ransom from devel-opers arriving to buy the lease in order to tear down the building for redevelopment.

Milt Levinson joins us, looms over us, a large man, tall. "I hear the Lithuanians didn't treat the Jews too well." He's talking about WWII.

Timothy Snyder, author of *Black Earth and Bloodlands*, provides the blood-chilling history of that murderous era. Yet Donna's mother risked prison, even death, when she rolled shelled boiled eggs onto stamped official documents and transferred the image to forged pass-ports for Jews to escape. Neither Donna nor I were called to perform acts of bravery in the face of life-and-death dangers that our parents faced. But in a moment of prosperity, we bought Israel Reconstruction bonds as an act of faith.

Today, we keep in mind that the monstrous crimes committed against Jews in the twentieth century have no parallel in history, or cur-rent events. Israel has every right to defend itself from enemies seeking to destroy it, though that right doesn't justify state-sponsored retribution inflicted on innocent civilians living in neighboring countries.

But neither genocide nor geopolitics keeps Milt's attention for long. We're going to look at the carpet-mill offerings tomorrow. The new look is plush. The colors are jewel tones. Milt tells us of a carpet mill he's signing on, "at lower price points."

39

THE CHALLENGES OF FAILURE DRAW MY ATTENTION TO another nonfiction subject. A literary agent offers mild encouragement. Much would depend, he says, "on the quality of the interviews and the insights provided." I'm looking into the burgeoning market for business opportunities advertised in classified print ads that were then available before migrating to the Internet.

Survey after survey lists the wish "to own a business" at the top of many kindred wishes such as being your own man or woman. Deep within our psyche we've adopted a mythology of individualism and a charismatic belief in the virtues of economic independence. A belief that has grown baroque, large enough to include Norman Rockwell's barbershop and Steve Jobs, homespun and Italian silk.

I began writing *Car Palace* before the Second Gilded Age of billionaires came clearly into view. Though Thomas Jefferson declared that "our creator made earth for the use of the living and not the dead ... one generation of men cannot foreclose or burthen its use to another," the extravagantly wealthy today are attempting to accomplish just that. The country that George Washington fought for, and ideas that Jefferson and Hamilton fought over, is much troubled. My book changes as I change, as my reading pleasures change, and as new information comes to light.

After several rounds of rewriting *Car Palace* I've amped up the personal, and cut back on the financial details—the amounts of money that I worried over, studied, projected on spreadsheets to justify loans now seem irrelevant in a financial world so altered that lifelong communists are also billionaire capitalists abusing local labor so their children can buy Lamborghinis to drive to school in America.

Things are in flux, class animosities rage.

Large companies used to *train* American workers, such as me. Rather than go through that commitment to teach and train each new generation of Americans they now find it more profitable to hire lower-wage employees overseas. Shockingly, even some Disney World workers have been thrown under the wheels of globalization, fired with termination packages that demanded confidentiality but required them to train their special visa lower-wage, subcontinent replacements. Walt Disney must be spinning in his grave. The company he founded, along with Snow White, Donald Duck, Micky Mouse and Pluto, appear to have no qualms doing business with totalitarian Communist regimes.

Many American companies no longer believe in investing in American workers, or even investing in America. They buy back their own company stock to *reduce* investment in American industry. A number of them evade American taxes with clever "inversion" strategies that allow them to buy smaller companies overseas, but structure the deal as if they themselves had been bought out, and then claim quasi-phony overseas headquarters to cut their US taxes. But they remain to do business in America, protected by American laws, American military, American infrastructure, and American freedom, without having to pay their fair share for American citizenship. They are architects of disloyalty, undermining America, our freedoms, our democracy, our hopes, and even our future.

The gig economy pitched to us as the footstool of entrepreneurship—no benefits, no vacation, no overtime pay, no family leave, no childcare, no healthcare insurance, no retirement either—is a disaster for future American generations. We're facing a democracy debased, a country where our creativity, work and productivity produces staggering wealth at the top that stagnates among the wealthy.

American corporations, though always legally empowered to be ruthless in the pursuit of profit, were once run by company chiefs who believed that they were Americans. No more, or at least not as much. Main Street entrepreneurs will never earn more than a sliver of the money these globalized accidents of history earn: the men and women who were at the right place and time to take advantage of science, new technology, demographics, financial deregulation, lower taxes, globalization, crippled unions, and the North American Free Trade Agreement, to seize for themselves staggering sums of money through the destruction of American jobs, and the hollowing-out of the middle class.

And if you're into very big money as one of the top-earning CEOs today, you've also earned enough money to buy a pulpit carved out of bullshit to claim that not only do you make a profit for your shareholders, you're also building a culture for customers and employees that fosters love, while you save the world.

But I'm located on Main Street and from this vantage point I see small-business owners, salaried and hourly employees, pocket entrepreneurs, the salt and bread of enduring American work and energy. They build the roads, serve in the military, dream up inventions, opportunities, careers, they build and sell products, they innovate whenever a new idea comes along, and they typically risk all they are, and own, and want to be, to try something new. They are our strength, the combat team to clean-up after our financial elites' countrywide failures.

The middle and working class does the work, the wealthy get to play. The hideous business motto "He who dies with the most toys wins" is no longer waiting in the wings. We're living it in this very moment. William Butler Yeats has put it another way: "We have fed the heart on fantasies / The heart has grown brutal from the fare."

40

I'S THE END OF A TOURIST AGENT'S IDEAL SEASON IN SEATTLE, the one you see in brochures with a snowcapped Mount Rainier painted sunny, the Puget Sound sparkling and dotted with sailboats. Our carpet stores are in the past, the printing store shows more signs of prospering: traffic is up, the number of customers increase, and the average sale is up. Once again the business is a jewel. I call Bollinger, "I haven't received my copy of the lease extension amendment." He agrees it's time.

In a flurry of notes, phone calls, we resolve minor points of disagreement. The lease and addendum, when finally signed by Bollinger and his wife signing personally, and as president of his corporation, and Donna and me, all twenty-eight pages initialed by us, and the lessee's payments personally guaranteed by Mike Lane, leave us more tired than elated.

Lexus construction takes off and I take off for another writers' conference. On the second evening into the Mount Holyoke conference I take advantage of the three-hour difference between the east and west coast to call the architect from a phone booth tucked in the narrow hallway. "What's happening?" I say. The casualness in my voice is an old habit, the coloring of insouciance. In my heart I hold apocalypse, the death of financial independence, unforeseen construction problems, growing disputes.

"Well, I don't know."

I clutch the phone tighter. "What don't you know?"

"Jeff says they found some peat bog." Jeff is the construction superintendent. If you're not a gardener, peat bog is bad news on a construction site. I prop a knee against a corner of the narrow booth, squeezing myself smaller.

"It's in the southeast corner, can't tell how large yet."

The peat bog might catapult our construction costs. I've had ten test holes dug across the lot by a soils engineer and five more holes underneath the proposed foundations. To get to load-bearing soil we had to dig as deep as fourteen feet below grade. The weather, so far, has been ideal. One of the driest springs and summers in years. Wonderful weather, except now we have peat bog.

"We're not building anything in that corner," I say. "They can pave right over it."

"Ed, the stuff won't hold paving. It's soupy."

I imagine the swelling waves, the crumbling asphalt, Lexus automobiles half-buried in a scene from a disaster movie. There's hardly enough space for the dealership to start with. We can't afford the lost land.

The telephone booth provides an illusion of privacy. A woman wants to use the phone. I see her running shoes, pink laces. Her foot is tapping. She wants to reach a boyfriend? A husband? Her children?

"I wish someone would have thought to check it out," I say.

That should have been me. Inexperience is expensive.

We're into it. I'm sounding snappy and quick-talking, too. "A'right, I'll call Jeff at the site and see what he says." I hang up. I let the woman use the phone. When she's finished I call Jeff at the construction site.

He answers. I picture him leaning over the drafting table in the small dusty mobile van he's hauled onto the site to serve as a field office. A clutter of tools, a battered chair—these are the amenities. He's dark haired, friendly, and probably without patience for writing misfits, among whom I've cast my lot.

"What's happening?" I say. I want him to say "not much," the pleasant absence of drama, the dullness of progress well planned and advancing.

"Hauling some peat," Jeff says. No muss, no fuss, almost bored. He displays his knowledge confidently.

"How many cubic yards?" I ask. I'm aligning the beads, my abacus working.

He gives me a number.

"Are you sure?" I'll take any number so long as it's firm. Please, no slippage, not here. My margin between being a local penny-ante developer and financial despair is as thin as the pages of a paperback book.

"Maybe a bit more," Jeff says. A calculated guess. He's eager to get back to his work.

"Can you use any of it at the site?"

"No."

It costs money to truck material away, and more money to truck material in. The dollars add up, as they always do. Two months into construction I've spent nearly the entire contingency fund, with most of the work remaining. And, no, Jeff can't use the peat; maybe he can fill a few flowerbeds, nothing more. I surrender my phone to another person waiting to use it, and join the writers' discussion in the main room.

A woman describes how she swiped a romance writer's purple prose to use in a satire. Amidst joviality and wine, she tells her story with great innocence and gusto. I'm a little out of it, still mired in peat bog. The communal decision quickly comes down to "change the words." There are no exceptions, except, well, there are so many exceptions: quoting, paraphrasing, homage, attribution, and especially the process of intimately absorbing another work that engages you and colors your own style. The writer decides to write her own sample of purple. A quick moral victory, so clearly defined.

The right thing to do is to notify the bank of the cost overrun and get its approval. But my bankers weren't so sure about making the loan in the first place. They could use one of several loan provisions to cancel their commitment and pull up stakes. Why give them a problem, and me a headache? My cash was always inadequate. The down payment wrapped around the value of the land.

The mechanics of construction loans are straightforward. The commercial real-estate bankers in the Northwest don't go to the same breakneck banking schools as do the freewheeling Wall Street bankers. Our bank has imposed a tapestry of limitations and conditions before they will approve the money draws. An independent construction-inspection service has to verify the contractor's estimates of completed construction before the bank will advance money.

Quite reasonably, the banker wants to see that there is enough money in the amount authorized to complete the building. Were it not so, the city wouldn't grant an occupancy permit. The tenant couldn't move in, nor pay rent, which would probably mean that the banker would become the reluctant owner of a vacant unfinished building. All this is so logical and orderly, prudent, that I would be pleased to put my savings account in the bank's care.

At the moment there's this other problem: The bank has not advanced its first draw. With no money advanced, a single word from a single nervous subcontractor placing a lien on the property could shut down the project.

Literary ambitions aside, I'm consumed by my worst fears—I might be ejected from the real-estate game before I have a chance to play. This explains, I think, why I'm only half-hearing Peter Viereck, the visiting poet at our Mount Holyoke conference, explain enthusiastically that iambic pentameter offers the very rhythm of life, the ebb and flow, the sudden surge of life carrying us further. He reads his metered lines, versified in a complex scheme from *Archer in the Marrow*. I think of an ornate bone carving, multiple lines of receding figures, chariots, clouds, warriors, maidens, and deer. I'm committed to Western traditions, but I wonder what someone from China or Borneo or Lapland would say about his life rhythm.

I've been of two minds for a long time, pushing for financial security from reluctant enterprises. Donna and I could represent the three generations John Adams described, but all of them packed into a single life: the greengrocer immigrant polishing apples to feed our children, hoping to send them to college, a professional corporate man a thread removed from the cozy levers of power, and now, as if reincarnated too quickly to grasp the changes, a writer, luxuriating in the heartbeat of iambic pentameter.

But even among congenial writers, on an evening warm with fellowship, my inner third generation lags as I get back to business. The key is the first bank draw. After it's released, the relationship changes between banker and borrower. Just like a book advance offered to a new author, the first construction advance is a tangible bet riding on the builder-developer's success.

I need to have the bank fund the first draw before I parade my disagreeable candor by identifying cost overruns. With a lack of subtlety that would distress me if it were laid out on a page for analysis, I find a loophole, a technicality. I ask the contractor not to submit the change orders to the bank. He would be paid later, from rents. This is between him and me, I say. I'll pay the cost overrun from Bollinger's rents after he moves in. The contractor agrees.

My conscience resisting me, I speak to the banker as if untroubled, and the bank releases the first draw. The engineers are paid miscellaneous fees, and the contractor has the money to pay his subcontractors. The architect receives his customary fee. I have peace of mind until the next draw.

When I read about technical violations of this or that statute, this or that rule, agreement or regulation, I rarely think of gross malfeasance. Most people in management know what they're doing, sometimes innocently, sometimes willfully, but they know, or at least suspect that a corner is being cut in a complex situation. It also happens that some of us are utterly naïve, but what comes to my mind are people of good will who stretch technicalities to close the gap.

The businesspeople who read this know of what I speak. The writers and artists bent on starting a business to support an unprofitable art habit have something to learn—commercial surfaces are thin, even fragile, and may collapse unexpectedly.

41

AFTER I RETURN FROM MOUNT HOLYOKE, THE CONTRACTOR calls me to the site. We study the architectural working drawings. I see a mirage of light-blue lines. He's thinking of material facts. We're working with a friendly conversational closeness, not every change is set down on paper, but the old traditions still reside in me. I insist that from now on I must have a change order for whatever needs to be done outside the contract. I'm not an experienced developer. I have no feel for alternatives. The documents are my refuge. Along with my fear that the project is slipping outside my control is a reluctance to become doctrinaire. We've plowed through the entire contingency fund, and now gone beyond it. "I hope we don't have any more surprises," I say. That's the contractor's hope, too. But neither one of us can control the earth and the sky and the weather.

"Well, uhh, I wanted to talk to you about that," the contractor says. "It looks as if we'll need to truck in more fill."

"You said the structural fill was the last of it." I must sound harassed.

I feel harassed. We get along, even like each other. The contractor doesn't like this conversation any more than I do.

"We're missing about six feet on the lower site level," he says. "Hard to tell how that'll affect us." The earthworks subcontractor, sensing our financial weakness, insists on getting paid for all the work immediately, before moving another load. If we don't pay him, he's ready to file a lien against the property. Once a lien is filed, the banker cannot advance additional construction money until the lien is paid off. I break the news to the mortgage banker gently, by phone. I'll need more money, implying that it isn't much to worry over now that I'm dealing in millions. "We have to deliver the building to Bollinger by September 1st."

"Ed," the banker replies with a hint of testiness. "We have to get you from here to September 1st." The lending rules are firm. The loan officer must show his superiors that there's enough the money to complete the scheduled work. Future rents are not an acceptable source.

Once again the project is foundering.

I look around for my missing clout and find instead another useful technicality—there's the $40,000 in the construction loan to pay the real-estate agent. If we remove this amount from the loan package, and push it back into the months when Bollinger starts to pay rent, we would have enough construction money to finish the building without another loan increase. The banker winks at the proposed solution. I tell the real-estate agent he'll have to wait a couple more months to receive his commission. Two technicalities, two sets of partners, two solutions: the first with the contractor to continue our funding, now with the real-estate man and the banker. This is Main Street, holding on as best as we can, racing to complete the building.

Meanwhile, my application to the MFA program at the University of Arizona in Tucson is in the works. Based on a writing sample, several recommendations, and an interview, I'm hoping to be accepted as a full-time student.

To better my chances I meet with the creative writing program director Steve Orlen. He's a warm man and a fine poet. He informs me that very few students my age gain admission to graduate school writing programs. If accepted, I'd be displacing some future aspiring and much younger writer, possibly another fabulous writer like David Foster Wallace, author of *Infinite Jest*, a University of Arizona alumnus.

I try to make a good impression, and casually mention my Eastern European roots, but I gloss over my business experience, a potential turnoff among the literati. It doesn't matter that at first I lived with my parents in a tenement that had no bathtub or shower. We used a metal tub, and my father with his larger knowledge of Rome and Pompeii would take me each week to the communal showers at the Y. Nor does it matter that I'm the kid who diligently fished for coins dropped out of reach through steel grates in city sidewalk openings—using a piece of chewy and warm bubble gum stuck to a stone on a string lowered six feet down. None of this matters because some at school will see me as a privileged middle-aged baby boomer. I would be paying out-of-state tuition, a hefty prosperous sum. I'm very late confronting the life passions that saw Jimi Hendrix, Janis Joplin, Jim Morrison, Kurt Cobain, and the Rolling Stones's Brian Jones dead of self-inflicted suffering, all at the age of twenty-seven. To smooth what's possibly a rough patch, I mention Sherwood Anderson, who wrote *Winesburg, Ohio*.

He was a businessman, too. "He had a nervous breakdown in order to become a writer."

Orlen looks concerned. "We don't want you doing that."

His office measures six or seven feet by nine—a shelf, an old desk holding a computer, two chairs discharged from government service several generations earlier—a space reflective of the bargain one makes with the arts to enter the world of the mind without limit.

"I'm into new beginnings," I say.

"Few of us know when those arrive."

The director is my age. He's not into ageism, and I'm getting a fair hearing. He pushes back from the cluttered desk involuntarily. "That's mostly what we do here," he says. "The beginnings, the endings." He's a graduate of University of Massachusetts Amherst and the Iowa Writers' Workshop. His poetry books are dedicated to a long gathering of friends.

He explains, "Much of the learning takes place outside the class, over coffee, meeting friends. Half the students are teachers to the undergraduates here; they know each other, talk in the hallways. Many of us have small kids. It's hard to break in. You have to be aggressive."

I bask in his concern, pleased that my business background has been worn smooth enough for him to fear that I might be too timid to make friends at school.

I'm attempting another border crossing. How clumsy will I be? He's trying to make it easier for me. The program historically accepts a small percentage of applicants. Many students have attended the finest Ivy League undergraduate colleges. I had always wanted to go away to college, live on campus, or nearby. An experience our children had enjoyed. But going away to college was a middle-class luxury outside my parents' means.

Donna's experience was worse. She got tagged as a working-class immigrant girl. Her high-school guidance counselor discouraged her from applying to college. Her parents didn't think it was necessary either. They preferred to spend their educational support money on her younger brother. Cultural sexism aimed at immigrant girls was part of our upbringing.

The question confronting her and me: how would I fit in if the University of Arizona accepts my application to graduate school? I'm twice the age of most grad students. Some say that any job that requires a change of clothes should be viewed with deep suspicion. I've changed my work clothes many times, and now that I'm applying for the job of student I need one more change. A car, in some respects, is like a piece of clothing. I buy the least expensive stick-shift economy car to drive to school in case I'm accepted. Donna christens it Tin Lizzy, not a car to attract attention alongside students saddled with debt.

42

THE FAA HASN'T YET WEIGHED IN ON THE BOMB SCARE THAT closed the Sea-Tac terminal on account of my son's explosive souvenir. This from a citizen writing to the editor of *The Seattle Times*: "I hope that charges are filed against the student responsible. Stupidity is not a justifiable excuse for violating international air safety." This from the director of Andrew's school attempting to placate a man who wants to sue for damages for his emotional distress: "The student's action was based on naïveté rather than maliciousness ... We have cooperated fully with the federal agencies which have pursued this matter." And this follow-up bomb headline: "Bomb! Well, sort of – war relic clears out terminal at Sea-Tac."

Andrew's lawyer sends a letter to the FAA special agent: "Andrew has certainly learned his lesson from the confusion, embarrassment, and problems resulting from his actions. Others have noted the irony that Andrew was one of the most rule-conscious, pro-American kids on the tour. In short, I can assure you that he will not make another mistake like this." A fellow student sends a letter defending Andrew: "None of us regarded the shell as potentially dangerous."

And finally this letter from the manager of the Enforcement Litigation Branch, Office of the Chief Counsel, US Department of Transportation, Federal Aviation Administration, addressed to Andrew: "Under the facts and circumstances of this case, it appears that your assertions, that you did not know and should not have known that the object was an explosive projectile, is reasonable. Please be advised that the Federal Aviation Administration has determined that initiation of legal enforcement action for violations of the Hazardous Material Regulations ... is not warranted in this case."

Words cannot describe our relief.

We're on the last lap to deliver Bollinger's car palace on time for him to join the Lexus national launch. We're wondering once again what to do with the printing store, a perennial question: to keep it or sell it?

And we're facing another problem, my brother, though sanguine and contemplative in his priestly calling, sees his health declining. A pastor in Mexico City has turned him into a commissioned salesman paid on the basis of the number of Masses he holds and the quantity of blessings he dispenses. The union of capitalism and Christianity can be demonstrably odd, even monstrous on occasion. There are no fair-trade employment contracts if you're working for God. The cardinal of his diocese flies in a piloted helicopter to check on God's domain. My brother can't afford a car. As age and ill health take an increasing toll on my brother's pastoral energies, his income decreases to the point he can't buy healthy food to stay well. (The pastor always ate well.) Donna and I become my brother's keeper for the next twenty years, to the end of his life. Indifferent to these future events, the characters in my novel are getting on with their lives and their future looks promising, just as it takes a dive for us.

Our printing store shows a sudden mysterious sales decline. I don't know how to break the bad news to Donna. Cass, unsure why Donna and I are in a huddle, comes over to tell us how well things are going. I explain the sales drop. Cass says it's only temporary. She goes off to help a customer. Donna, the Lady of the Second Chance, also the third chance, and the fourth chance, says to me, "I told you. I told you we can depend on Cass."

But a few days later a customer confirms my worst suspicion: Cass appears to be siphoning off our customers to set up her own independent printing brokerage business. We've trained her, taught her the printing business. Her overhead is lower. As a printing broker she doesn't have to rent an office location or set up shop, and she doesn't have to pay the employer's share of employees' social security, unemployment and disability taxes. While pleading with our customers to leave us, she also earns a salary from us. From her point of view, what's not to like?

Donna's expression goes flat, her eyes glaze over. "I've been betrayed, humiliated."

To boost our sagging mood, I retrieve a photograph celebrating the Lexus groundbreaking months earlier. The sign reads: "FUTURE HOME OF LEXUS." A huge white and yellow striped circus tent has been erected to shelter a catered sit-down lunch to thank the gathered vendors, contractors, the mayor, and the council members. I'm startled and pleased to see Donna and me looking so young in the photograph, our faces unlined. I have an American flag pinned to my lapel. Bollinger has a big smile and wonderful teeth and a white hard hat. Next to him his wife is beautifully dressed in a white high-neck pleated dress and a luminous orange sweater, but no hard hat—her hair looks great.

Mike Lane stands with his wife. They're both wearing hard hats. I'm next, and Donna is at the front of the line. No hard hats for us—we like our hair exposed. A pile of dirt has been pushed into a clichéd photo-op position. Unlike everyone else holding individual silver-plated shovels poised to dig, Donna and I hold only one shovel, our hands intertwined. We're not to the manor born. The silver in our hands may be fleeting.

We thank the graces for our mostly good fortune. The Lexus building is on schedule to receive its city occupancy permit. The sale of the printing store attracts several buyers.

My graduate school application is still pending, though acceptance remains iffy. We inquire about joining the Peace Corps as volunteers, hoping to find another door through which we can step into a new beginning. The days move faster, the anxieties of life continue, steeped in the ecology of transitions, and the structure of uncertainty.

Nathanael West, writing in *The Day of the Locust*, warns: "They were savage and bitter, especially the middle-aged and the old, and had been made so by boredom and disappointment." Not us, not yet, not ever we hope.

The mail arrives late in the afternoon. Donna shows me an envelope from the University of Arizona in Tucson. I don't want to deal with the rejection, and ask Donna to put it aside. Instead, she opens the envelope and starts reading:

"I'm pleased to inform you that the Creative Writing faculty has read your work and accepted you into the MFA program. Signed by Steve Orlen." Her eyes brighten.

"What?" I ask.

"You're a writer?"

"I hope so."

And so we move on.

I invoked Dorothy at the beginning of this memoir. She danced and sang along the Yellow Brick Road in a journey of self-discovery on the way to see the wonderful Wizard of Oz. The Cowardly Lion accompanied her, the brainless Scarecrow, and the Tin Man, too. The Lion found courage, the Tin Man discovered his heart, and Scarecrow got smarter.

Dorothy is safe back in Kansas. Donna and I are home, too.

Robert Frost wrote about the two roads that diverged in the yellow wood, both equally fair. We're now on the road less traveled by, a road we did not choose earlier, the one we hope will make all the difference.

POSTSCRIPT

THE LEXUS AUTOMOBILE BECAME AN ASTONISHING SUCCESS among industry critics and car buyers alike. Bollinger sold many cars, overextended himself financially, and then he sold his dealership to a West-Coast megadealer. The Bollingers divorced. Donna and I sold the printing company. Donna created a magically diverse and flowering garden in the Sonora Desert to serve as a refuge for butterflies, bats and birds alike. I earned a Master of Fine Arts from the University of Arizona and published three novels as Holland Kane. including *Morning Light*. A tale for our culturally divided times.

In the novel, David, stunned by his mother's grave illness, looks to his mother's friend, Emily, for comfort. She's a young contemporary dancer on the brink of wide public acclaim, but held back by despair. Her pious, loving, Catholic, husband condemns her use of birth control. Challenged to save her imperiled marriage, her friendship with David tumbles into unprotected one-night passionate sex. Pregnant, she rejects abortion, hopes to stay married, and refuses her husband's demand that she hook up with an adoption agency.

ACKNOWLEDGMENTS

Donna and I are grateful to have met so many others on the roads we have chosen to travel, and grateful for all the help we received, the sights we've seen and the things we did together.

I need to thank the many passionate teachers I met in my trek across the literary landscape, and the institutions that offered them a home: St. Ambrose School, Brooklyn Technical High School, the City College of New York, Seattle University, the University of Arizona, the University of Iowa Writers' Workshop for a semester spent with Frank Conroy, and much gratitude too for classes I attended at Temple University, The New School and New York University. I need to thank The Writers Room in Manhattan for a desk that allowed me to work peacefully, also the New York State Board of Regents for a scholarship, and the GI Bill of Rights for help in paying for graduate school.

On the business side, I wish to thank the late Bollinger and his associates for our engagement in the practice of commerce on Main Street. He allowed me to record him, spoke without inhibition, and arranged interviews with his then-wife, his father, and several others—edited here for content and brevity.

We were not solo travelers. Many individuals were indispensable. They are the large community of talented business professionals working on Main Street, accountants and lawyers, bankers, contractors, small-business owners, and real-estate agents, including Marty Rood, a former auto dealer, who guided me toward a history of Highway 99. I also owe a debt of gratitude to John Wahl who has kept the car palace in excellent repair, and to our wonderful attorney, Shannon Sperry, who kept Donna and me out of trouble.

I wish to thank The Editorial Department and its publishing professionals: Morgana Gallaway for publishing oversight and interior design, Doug Wagner for copyediting, and the meticulous Amanda Bauch for proofreading. Other publishing professionals have helped, among them Beth Jusino, Lonnie Ostrow, Karin Bilich and Rachel Anderson.

I'm grateful also to friends who were willing to read this memoir in its earlier drafts—Edmundas Adomaitis, Michael Chittock, Kelly Leslie (who also designed the book's cover), Paul Ivey, Mary Rogers, Gary Swimmer, Tim Vanderpool, and Kim Walter.

Though our children, Andrew Trimakas and Lisa Thew, were young in the period covered by the memoir, and have moved on to their own passionate adult encounters with life, they remain in our hearts and our memories, with the hope that joy follows them wherever life leads.

This journey into The Great American Experience couldn't have been traveled without Donna. I owe a debt to my wife beyond gratitude. We've taken a road paved with many highs and several lows, dancing over cobblestones and dodging noisy traffic, braving intersections marked by despair to reach several crossroads offering hope—a journey of love. As long as there are arts to practice and gardens to grow, and breath continues, we'll keep on moving.

A NOTE ABOUT THE AUTHOR

Gediminas Trimakas spent his childhood in Europe and teenage years in New York City. He holds a Master of Fine Arts in fiction, a graduate degree in finance, and served with distinction in the US Army Signal Corps. As a *Sonora Review* editor he published prose by Maxine Kumin, the United States poet laureate and Pulitzer Prize winner. He wrote three novels under a pen name—*Morning Light* won praise from Kirkus Reviews and Publisher's Weekly. He lives with his wife in the Pacific Northwest.

Visit him online at WWW.TRIMAKASAUTHOR.COM

Winter Reeds

by GEDIMINAS TRIMAKAS as Holland Kane

"Kane spins a fascinating web of discoveries and intrigue, and the surprises don't stop until the very end."
— *Kirkus Reviews*

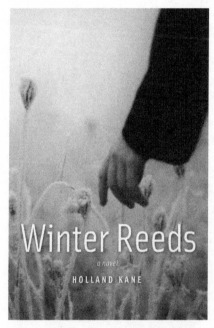

Documentary filmmaker Mike Harrison moves from New York City to a remote Northwest town to research an infamous car dealership fire. The generation-old, unsolved arson left two people dead, and if Mike can solve the mystery, he'll have a career-making movie. He's distracted though, by beautiful Katie Ames, a fellow New Yorker who's come to Hallmark County with her mentally handicapped brother, to piece together their own complicated past.

Katie's dating an architect who was tangled up in the dealership arson. The man is obsessed with Katie, and threatens her when she tries to break up with him. The next morning, the police find his dead body.

Mike and Katie are outsiders in a town where the popular Sheriff Trout is a law unto himself, and citizens live under constant surveillance ... But there's a story to be told: one that ties the arson, the dead architect, the sheriff, and Katie's missing family together into a devastating small-town scandal.

Winter Reeds Print ISBN 978-0-9858293-0-8
Winter Reeds Digital ISBN 978-0-9858293-1-5

Morning Light

by GEDIMINAS TRIMAKAS as Holland Kane

"A story of loss, ethics, and forbidden love."
— Kirkus Reviews

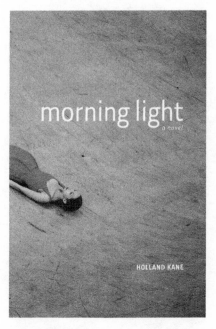

Seventeen-year-old David's mother is dying from cancer when he turns to her best friend—the beautiful, emotional dancer Emily—for comfort, which one afternoon turns into passion. Their affair is brief, but it comes with a consequence: she becomes pregnant.

Emily's devout Catholic husband has stopped sleeping with her in a dispute about birth control, so there's nowhere for the lovers to hide. Results crash around like lightning strikes as David tries to woo Emily, and Emily tries to hang on to it all: her imperiled marriage, her breakout career as a choreographer, her unborn child, and David.

As the award-winning novelist Carol Orlock observes: "In this exploration of a modern woman's search for love and fulfillment, Holland Kane sheds light on the dark places our dreams can carry us, places we never meant to go."

Morning Light Print ISBN 978-0-9858293-3-9
Morning Light Digital ISBN 978-0-9858293-4-6

DEER CREEK

by GEDIMINAS TRIMAKAS as Holland Kane

Author Holland Kane returns to the northwestern area he first described in the acclaimed novel Winter Reeds *for a new story about ambition, love, and secrets that bind them together.*

Two sisters, Rikki and Abbey—Rikki given away at birth and lost in the foster care system, Abbey pampered with love and privilege—become friends, but don't know they are related, or why they feel a deep bond.

Around them, their home of Deer Creek is buckling. Rikki's lover, the deputy mayor, wields his privately funded SWAT team as a weapon in class warfare. A health report threatens to uncover a scandal lurking in the local world-famous tourist destination spa. Everyone has a secret to hide. A story about ambition, love, lies and government misconduct.

> "In a time of universal deceit,
> telling the truth becomes a revolutionary act."
> —George Orwell

Deer Creek Print ISBN: 978-0-9858293-6-0
Deer Creek Digital ISBN: 978-0-9858293-7-7

CPSIA information can be obtained
at www.ICGtesting.com
Printed in the USA
BVOW11*0930130517

483300BV00001B/1/P